Centre Stage

'Jeannette Nelson's revelatory relationship to language is, quite simply, life-changing . . . Her meticulous, empowering approach is irresistible and inspiring.'
Simon Godwin

'Jeanette Nelson is, for me, the foremost practitioner in her field. Her ability to nurture and empower through truth, rigour, intelligence and wit is one of the great unsung bedrocks of our world-leading theatre. This insightful and overdue book is an illumination of her unique craft, as accessible to the public as it is invaluable to the professional.'
Rufus Norris, Artistic Director, National Theatre

'Jeannette has been a huge influence on my directing practice. The opportunity to witness her practice, wisdom and humanity in the rehearsal room as a young director was both inspiring and mind-expanding. Her ability to unlock text and release the very best from actors, directors and therefore the productions has been a vital contribution to the industry. For Jeannette to share her experiences and industry-wide respected intellect more widely is a true gift for us all.'
Indhu Rubasingham, Artistic Director Designate, National Theatre

Centre Stage

*Lessons from Actors on the
Art of Charisma*

Jeannette Nelson

Cornerstone Press

1 3 5 7 9 10 8 6 4 2

Cornerstone Press
20 Vauxhall Bridge Road
London SW1V 2SA

Cornerstone Press is part of the Penguin Random House group of companies
whose addresses can be found at global.penguinrandomhouse.com.

First published by Cornerstone Press in 2024

www.penguin.co.uk

A CIP catalogue record for this book is available from the British Library.

ISBN 9781847943354

Typeset in 12/17pt Dante MT Std by Jouve (UK), Milton Keynes
Printed and bound in Great Britain by Clays Ltd, Elcograf S.p.A.

The authorised representative in the EEA is Penguin Random House Ireland,
Morrison Chambers, 32 Nassau Street, Dublin D02 YH68

Penguin Random House is committed to a sustainable future
for our business, our readers and our planet. This book is made
from Forest Stewardship Council® certified paper.

*To the many, many actors and directors from whom
I have learned my trade and especially to the wonderful
actors who contributed to this book.*

CONTENTS

INTRODUCTION

I will never forget the first time I saw Al Pacino rehearse a scene. It was 2004, and I was voice coach on the film of *The Merchant of Venice* directed by Michael Radford, with Al playing the role of Shylock. From the moment he arrived in the rehearsal studio, he was in character. He wore black clothes, including a long, black coat, and carried his body in a downward leaning posture, his eyes mainly looking to the floor. But when he lifted them, he had the most penetrating gaze. Even in that first rehearsal he was astonishingly powerful, and the young actors in the scene with him appeared almost paralysed by that power.

I soon learned just how committed Al is to his work. When it came to filming, his intense energy, focus, creativity and stamina paid tribute to his training and his early career in theatre. He would ask for take after take of each of his scenes until he was satisfied that he had offered up everything he could, resulting in a very human, complex and compelling portrayal of his character. This fascinating presence was not something that only emerged on screen, however; he had the same quality in real life. One evening after rehearsals, he invited us to drinks at his apartment in New York. In that relaxed setting, at home with fellow professionals and friends, he was a charming host and as charismatic as he is on camera. Like many of the actors I have met, his personality wasn't forceful or dominating; it emerged from an understated self-confidence and self-reliance that made him very attractive. When I spoke to him, his attention seemed to be entirely on me. He was really listening to what I said.

When you encounter very charismatic people like Al, it is tempting to assume that it is something that has come to them naturally, that some of us are simply better at holding people's attention than others. There might be some truth in that idea. But observing Al Pacino and other great actors makes you realise that their charisma – in performance and in person – often comes from their commitment to their work: the craft and art of acting. And it is a craft we can all learn from.

This book is going to introduce you to some of the work I do with actors to help them communicate powerfully and charismatically. As a voice coach, my job is to help actors fulfil and maintain their potential as artists who are, above all, communicators. I will share with you some of the advice I give to them and the exercises I use to get the best out of their voices, their bodies and their scripts. Along the way, I will share some of their experiences with you – experiences that they were kind enough to share with me in my research for this book. By introducing you to the methods that actors use to communicate effectively, my hope is that you too will glean insights into how to perform with charisma in your own life.

ACTORS AS ARTISTS

Working with actors is a privilege. Being part of the creative process of artists has led me to work on some of the most demanding stages in the world, everywhere from the National Theatre, the Royal Shakespeare Company, Shakespeare's Globe Theatre, Sydney Theatre Company and in most of London's beautiful, iconic West End theatres, to school halls, warehouses, churches and even the Houses of Parliament. In many cases, I have been lucky enough to work with an actor from the very beginning of their artistic journey at drama school right through to the height of their profession.

During this time, I have had the pleasure of working with some of our most talented actors and, as any teacher will tell you, working with people of great talent and ability always teaches the teacher as much as the student. I

first understood how an actor can fill the National Theatre's Olivier stage by watching and listening to actors who
have performed there for years. I have learned how to help
actors with their vocal projection and clarity by working
alongside those who began their careers in regional rep-
ertory theatres in the 1950s. I have seen how an actor can
take an audience on a journey with clever, subtle shifts in
their body language that draw the audience's attention to
where they want it to go. Every day I see actors being so
free and flexible with their bodies, voices and minds that
you forget who they are; you only see and hear the character and the story being told.

In a career spanning over thirty years – twenty-five of
those at the National Theatre – my role has been to support actors from the first day of rehearsal to the day the
play closes. During the five or six weeks of rehearsal, I
work with them individually and in groups. My job in the
early stages is to check in with how comfortable they are
with their vocal technique and the vocal demands of the
play. We may do a voice 'workout', using some of the exercises I will be sharing with you in this book, which will
ensure they are heard clearly throughout the theatre.
When I'm not working with the actors directly, I attend
rehearsals to hear how their voice work is progressing and,
equally importantly, I listen to what the director is asking
them to do. Once the play begins preview performances –
when we have evening audiences but are still rehearsing

during the day – I lead pre-show voice warm-ups, and I attend performances to monitor the actors' audibility and clarity. After the Press Night, when the play has officially opened, I continue to lead regular warm-ups and keep my ear on the work by attending performances from time to time.

I also work with actors on the language of the script, especially if it is a classical or political play. An important part of my career has been to study the work of great playwrights, from the timeless classical plays of ancient Greece and Rome, through medieval mystery plays, Shakespeare and his contemporaries and the plays of the Restoration period, to the groundbreaking plays of Chekhov and Ibsen and right up to the present. From these great writers I have learned how stories in drama are told and how believable, truthful characters are formed. I have learned how language can be used, structured and spoken in ways that change people, situations and stories. From this study and my knowledge of the body and voice, I am able to work alongside actors and directors to support and develop the art they are making.

My job is twofold. First, I keep the actors' voices in shape and up to the task of performing night after night in theatres big and small. Second, I help them to recognise and understand the way the play is written, and to empower them to use the language in active and persuasive ways.

This book will offer you insights from both sides of my job: from the exercises I use to help actors warm up their voices before they go on stage and insights into how to feel in control in any room or on any stage, to the methods I use to help actors understand the most difficult scripts they are working with. In offering you these methods, my hope is that you will feel more confident 'performing' in your own life. This book will be particularly useful for anyone who is preparing to speak in front of a large group – perhaps you are getting ready to give a wedding speech, or have been working up to a crucial presentation in your job. Or maybe you need to deliver an important talk at a conference. In every case, this book will introduce you to exercises that will allow you to communicate clearly, confidently and – above all – charismatically.

However, the insights I can impart are not limited to big, set-piece speeches. You can also learn how to 'hold the room' in a conversation by the water cooler, at a dinner party, or in the pub. You can learn to feel more confident and comfortable socially by becoming aware of how your body and voice work, by listening to others more effectively and by becoming aware of the give-and-take of conversation, debate and argument. You can learn to use your voice more expressively as you read a bedtime story to your children or grandchildren, or share your views with your book club or study group. Charismatic communication is useful in every setting.

WHAT IS CHARISMA?

What is it that gives a person charisma? We recognise it when we see it; many actors exude it. It is that quality that draws us to somebody, that makes us want to listen to them and to be around them. It is a quality that can hold an audience, from the stage and in the boardroom; on the screen and in the office; at a party and at dinner.

It is also a quality that can be learned. Having trained young actors and then worked with them in professional theatre, I have seen them metamorphose from awkward teenagers to lovely, genuine, charismatic people – not just when they perform but in real life too. Most, though not all, actors train in drama school when they are in their late teens and early twenties; while there, they explore who they are and learn to have confidence in that person: an actor cannot transform into someone else if they don't know who they are in the first place. They also learn to present that person to the world. Actors have to constantly 'sell' themselves to get work. In most professions you might interview for a job every three to five years; actors audition for many jobs every year, and, if they are lucky, get two or three of them. Actors suffer performance anxiety as well as the blows of rejection, but they have to learn to manage these, to make sure they can perform at the peak of their ability. It is not easy to maintain charisma in the face of these challenges – but they do so through their understanding of their craft.

In the course of a life spent working with and teaching actors, I have come to conclude that charisma is made up of three powerful and dynamic qualities, which lie at the heart of this book: First, authenticity. Learning to develop charisma does not mean you will be artificial. Authenticity is very important to me, to actors and to the work we do together. My job as a theatre voice coach is to help the actors to free their voices so that they can respond to the characters and situations they are creating from a place of truth. If they are not truthful, the audience will soon spot it and they will not engage with the play or film. In fact, if they are not truthful, the actor would not get the job in the first place.

The same is true for you. If you try too hard to be liked, to please, to sound interesting or clever, your *inauthenticity* will show. You will probably be presenting some physical tension or be thought to be pushy. Your voice will give you away, as it will be harder for you to speak fluently, or to pace your delivery appropriately. Similarly, and maybe surprisingly, self-consciousness, shyness and anxiety can present as lack of interest or lack of intellect, which will also make you less likely to be trusted. If you are not brave enough to enter the room or to speak up, no one will know whether you are authentic or not in the first place. Authenticity, then, is the focus of the first two chapters of the book. In Chapter 1,

I explain the practicalities of using your body with ease, to help you to look and feel confident, and to enable you to breathe and speak freely, while in Chapter 2, I explain how your voice works, and show you how, by improving your breath, resonance, projection and clarity, you will come to communicate in a more authentic manner.

The second quality when it comes to charisma is authority. In this context, authority does not mean power in the competitive sense, but power in the sense of being trusted and believed. That comes from knowledge of your subject, of course, but it also comes from having the confidence and ability to speak about it fluently. There is technique involved in becoming this kind of authoritative communicator. Actors research the plays they perform in and the lives of the characters they play very thoroughly but their authority comes from the ability to communicate well and tell stories that we engage with and believe. Authority does not mean overconfidence or unearned respect. It comes from knowledge of yourself and your subject, and your ability to communicate clearly and effectively. That is why the next section of the book will focus on how taking control of the situation in which you are communicating can bolster your sense of authority. In Chapter 3, you will learn to develop control over the delivery of your material, and in turn to be expressive and engaging. And in Chapter 4, you will learn how to 'own' the room you are in, including when speaking on film or video.

Last, but by no means least, is eloquence. A beautiful word, even if some might feel it is a little old-fashioned. There's nothing antiquated about eloquence, however; it is fluent or persuasive speaking – as such, I consider it to be vital to modern life and it is certainly necessary to the world of plays and acting. Think of a scene from a play or television drama you have seen. You might already be thinking of well-known plays, like those of Shakespeare – Romeo persuading Juliet to kiss him at the party where they first meet, for example:

ROMEO: *Have not saints lips, and holy palmers too?*
JULIET: *Ay, pilgrim, lips that they must use in prayer.*
ROMEO: *O then, dear saint, let lips do what hands do:*
They pray: grant thou, lest faith turn to despair.

But you can also see eloquence in soap operas, where characters are constantly trying to persuade each other to support them, or fall in love with them, or help them to make money. We do the same in real life. Eloquence is the ability to affect people through persuasive language. It is used in politics, playwriting, storytelling, debate, argument, flirting, lovemaking and warmongering. It is one of the most powerful tools in the great communicator's toolkit. As such, the final chapter of the book focuses on eloquence. It examines useful rhetorical techniques, some

elements of storytelling and the textual analysis techniques used by actors every day.

Through these chapters, my hope is that you will be
able to develop a way of communicating that is at once
powerfully compelling and true to your character. By
bringing together authenticity, authority and eloquence
you will develop charisma. This book will show you how.

PART I
AUTHENTICITY

CHAPTER 1

YOUR BODY

Peter Forbes is an actor who has worked at the National Theatre on and off for about thirty years. Equally at home in comedy, straight drama and musical theatre, I have seen him play everything from heartbreaking spurned husbands to comedic British Army generals. Yet despite his successful career, Peter tells me that this ability to depict such a wide array of parts didn't come naturally. To convincingly portray these diverse parts, he first had to get to know himself.

'When I first started acting, as a child, just at school, I was fascinated by the idea that you were putting on a disguise and becoming someone else,' he says. 'I was a bit scared of the idea that you start with yourself. I think you have to be quite confident about yourself to do that.' And yet, with time, he came to realise that only by becoming relaxed about who you are can you learn to perform with authenticity. 'If I think about how my approach to acting has changed over thirty years, it's probably more of a stripping away than an adding.'

If you want to change the way you communicate, you too have to begin with a degree of 'stripping away'. You have to find out what your habits are, how they might interfere with your communication skills and how you can change them. Young actors arrive at drama school with the clothing, movements and attitudes of whatever group they had identified with at school or at home. Before starting their classes, they are usually asked to remove all jewellery, and for some classes to put on simple black clothing. This is a shedding of the outer layer that hides their true selves. It is symbolic of what they will be doing throughout their training: learning to know and be comfortable with who they are as individuals. This is what it means to be authentic; learning to be at ease with yourself, so others will be at ease with you too.

It all starts with finding physical ease. When I was teaching the student actors in the Drama Department of the Guildhall School of Music and Drama, the work on voice and movement were integrated; voice tutors used movement in voice classes and movement tutors used breath and sound in movement classes. That is because speaking is a physical activity: whatever you do with your body will affect your voice. It is part of why Guildhall focuses on training its students to be physically free, flexible and creative – the teachers in the movement department understand that this freeing work will also free the breath and release the areas of tension that can interfere with easy, free voices. It is also why, as a voice coach, I always begin my work with actors by considering how they use their bodies, and when we warm up the voice for performance, we always begin with some physical work.

In every case, the first step to authentic self-expression is to focus on your body. So that is where we will begin.

LEARNING TO BE PRESENT

One of the first things an actor learns at drama school is how to stand up, be still and just breathe. They are taught how to be present.

That might sound simple. In fact, it is one of the hardest things you can do: to let your guard down and simply present yourself to the world without inhibition. Life teaches us early on that we should conceal elements of ourselves. We learn how to protect ourselves from classroom bullies, or become one ourselves; we learn that it is safer to be one of the crowd and to behave and dress like everyone else; we look to blend into our 'tribe' in order to find safety in numbers. None of this invites us to hold our bodies in a way that is physically open. We develop physical habits, tensions and tics that form a barrier between the world and our true, vulnerable selves.

To begin your journey, then, you must consider your own physical habits. Many of the actors I have spoken to for this book have mentioned the importance of noticing, in minute detail, what their bodies are doing. Danny Sapani, an actor who has played leading roles at the National Theatre – as well as making many TV and film appearances, including in *Killing Eve*, *The Crown* and *Black Panther* – told me about watching himself on the director's monitor during the filming of a scene in the Sky television series *Penny Dreadful*. In the process of making a film, the director will want several 'takes' of each scene in order to get the right lighting or interpretation, and to film the scene from the perspective of each character, showing them both speaking and listening. In this particular scene, Danny's character had nothing to say and was sitting in the background, listening to the main protagonists. When he saw one of the takes played back, he realised that every tiny movement he'd made could be read as his thoughts: 'even the smallest movement of my finger had meaning,' he recalls. Seeing this, he was able to work with those tiny movements when they did the next take.

Actors need a high degree of awareness and control to be able to use the body so subtly. The starting point for many is the Alexander Technique – a way of being and moving that also contributes to good breathing and voice.

The technique was created by Frederick Matthias Alexander (1869–1955) working with his own voice and breathing, and he later developed it into a practice to improve the use of the whole body. It teaches us to recognise how the body reacts to the stresses of life and how to manage those reactions. Working with a practitioner, we can learn to observe our habitual body usage through observation in a mirror, and through small adjustments made by the practitioner. These adjustments are concerned with freeing us from the downward pull of gravity, which tends to make us compress our bodies and so restrict movement and breathing. We then learn to take these adjustments into our everyday life. The practice is generally taught as part of acting training in drama schools, and at the National Theatre there is a resident Alexander Technique teacher for the benefit of the actors.

My work is also informed by the Alexander Technique, and with this knowledge, I can help you to identify physical habits you might have that interfere with the free release of your voice. First, take a moment to think about how you habitually use your body. When you are standing with other people, do you automatically cross your arms over your chest? Is your chest collapsed, or do you always stand with your hands clasped in front of your groin or in your pockets? Are there situations when you find it hard to make eye contact with people or stoop because you feel too tall? On the other hand, do you stand or sit with your legs open wide? Is your chin raised high so that you appear to be looking down on the world? All the postures I have described are in some way protective or defensive, and are definitely not open. When you are anxious, you might instinctively try to make yourself smaller or unnoticeable. But the opposite doesn't give you charisma, either. Those of us who challenge the world by taking up a lot of space, standing wide, with the chest pushed forward, can be intimidating. This sort of posture is often perceived as bluff: pretending or hiding something by pushing our presence into the world rather than opening ourselves to it.

So, we're going to take a moment to observe and break down your physical habits. Go and stand in front of a mirror, a full-length one if possible. What do you look like? Try to take an objective look and see yourself as others do, or as you would if you were looking at someone else. Where are your protective or defensive tensions? How do you balance your weight?

Next, try imagining yourself in different scenarios: giving a wedding speech or a speech of thanks; entering a party or reception full of strangers; talking to your boss or an important client; leading a meeting or giving a presentation or a performance to a large audience. If you can, recreate the sort of postures you might find yourself taking in those different situations and think about or remember how you *feel*. Take your time so that you can notice what is happening in your body. How are you breathing? Are you taking small, shallow breaths or are you holding your breath? Notice if these postures make your body look stiff or closed off.

Even if you think you look and feel reasonably relaxed, can you notice the smallest of physical tensions? Where are they? Are your shoulders a little lifted or tense? Is your neck tight or stiff? How about your jaw or your face? Are your knees locked back? Do you look rather reluctant or apologetic or a bit too keen? Besides interfering with how you speak and move, these tensions can also send unhelpful messages to others. Even if you are bluffing confidence with a lifted chest or wide stance, postures that depend on tension do not draw people to you. The Alexander Technique teaches us that once we are aware of these tensions, we can make changes. We can choose to let our shoulders drop, or unlock our knees; to release the tension in our jaw or neck.

Now stand up straight with your feet no wider apart than your hips and with your knees unlocked – not bent, but just releasing your kneecaps and any tension in your thighs. This is important. Locking your knees can lock your whole body as it thrusts your weight backwards and the tightness of your legs means you lose flexibility. This tightness also has an adverse effect on your breathing as it sends tension into your lower back and therefore restricts the movement of your ribs, diaphragm and lungs. So release those knees and take a moment to notice how it feels.

Try going from tight knees to released knees a couple of times, and then consider your whole body to notice any changes. Once you've done this, try this exercise to release any tension that remains:

Exercise 1: To recognise and release physical tension

One way to remove any tension is to tighten and release your body one bit at a time. You could start at your feet and ankles, tightening and then releasing them a couple of times. Then move up to your calves, then your thighs, then your buttocks and hips followed by your abdomen. Then tighten and release around your ribs and your back, then work through your hands and your arms. Next, your chest and your shoulders, followed finally by your face and your neck. This exercise can also make you realise where you hold tension habitually, as those areas will already feel quite tight.

Alternatively, you can release tension by shaking out your body, bit by bit, starting with your hands and arms, then your feet and legs, then your torso, and then shaking every bit of your body at the same time. This is an exercise that actors often do in warm-up, or just before they go on stage.

I once worked with Claire, an employee at the National Theatre whose promotion meant she had to address the public from time to time. When we met to work on her delivery, she was clearly very anxious. As she stood at the podium to read her speech, she was gripping it with both hands and her knees were locked tight. This affected her whole performance. When she began to speak, her voice was monotone and she sounded breathy, having to take more breaths than were necessary. The first thing I asked her to do was to release her knees. Immediately, her whole body relaxed, she let go of the podium and she took a breath. I then asked her to shake out her body as suggested in the exercise opposite. She enjoyed the shake out; it made her laugh, and we began again.

When you've tried one of these releasing exercises, stand still and look at yourself again. Can you remember the feeling of ease after shaking or releasing tension? Can you resist going back into your old physical habits? If you can stand still with as little tension in your body as possible, your shoulders should have dropped and your face should look more relaxed, more open and accessible. Just as importantly, do you *feel* different? It is very possible that this open, uninhibited posture may make you feel that you are no longer in control: we often mistake familiar tension for readiness or alertness. But the contrary is true. In the words of Konstantin Stanislavski, the great, innovative Russian acting teacher who transformed

Western acting in the nineteenth and early twentieth centuries. 'At times of great stress it is especially necessary to achieve complete freeing of the muscles.' Physical tension will inhibit your movement, constrict your blood vessels and therefore reduce blood flow to your brain.

By noticing your habits, you can begin to embrace or, where necessary, change your physical demeanour. The experienced film, television and theatre actor Tamsin Greig told me about a method used by the director Stephen Frears, which she learned when performing in one of his films. Before filming a scene, it is normal for the actors and the director to do a short rehearsal for themselves and for the camera and lighting crew. Tamsin said that after their rehearsal, Stephen 'would stand in the middle of the set and say, "What's wrong with that?"' This sounded negative, she thought at first. But then she realised what he was getting at. He was encouraging actors to notice their behaviour, and ask: 'What would stop this plant from growing in the best way it can?'

You could take a similar approach to your development. By giving yourself moments to check in with your body, notice what you're doing, and perhaps say, 'what's wrong here?', you will retain your focus on your progress and learn to recognise how you can help yourself. This is the starting point for all the work in this book: understanding your body and noticing what it is doing.

GETTING INTO A NEUTRAL POSTURE

In theatre we talk a lot about different elements of the work being 'in the body'. Memorising lines; speaking from the belly; the characteristics of the person you are playing – we might describe any of them as being 'in the body'. Adjoa Andoh – an actor and director perhaps best known from her role as Lady Agatha Danbury in the TV series *Bridgerton* as well as her many roles at the National Theatre and Royal Shakespeare Company – told me that when she is preparing for a performance, she walks around the performance space beforehand until she feels physically at home there; until it's 'in the body'.

You could be forgiven for finding this phrase a little confusing. After all, aren't all of us 'in the body' all the time? But in theatre this term has a more specific meaning. We use this phrase as a shortcut indicating the way that actors have to feel at one with their whole body in order to communicate with authenticity, truthfulness and ease.

In this section, we'll move from noticing your physical habits to changing them, with a focus on how you too can get 'in the body'. That starts with posture. When I begin to work with actors on a particular role, or to warm them up before a performance, we always begin by getting into a neutral posture. It is a blank canvas upon which they will draw their character, or from which their character will emerge. Neutral isn't anonymous: it is them, but a version of them with as much unhelpful tension removed as possible. Debra Gillett, an actor I've worked with many times at the National Theatre, spoke about its power in building a convincing character. 'There may be a different way your character walks and uses their body,' she said, but 'it's important to begin with a neutral spine and stance, knees soft etc., and to then put in quirks for the character.'

You have already made the first step towards a neutral posture by releasing tension from your muscles. The second step is finding a good centre of balance. If your body is habitually off-centre, it will be much harder for you to be able to respond to situations quickly, and to free your voice. I remember having a conversation with a very experienced actress playing an important leading role. She was playing opposite a young actress, and she told me that she found it difficult to act with her. In dialogues, she said, the younger actress's responses were a bit late and they didn't have the lively give-and-take that the scenes required. Actors like to feel that they are bouncing off each other's energy when they act together – this is what gives life and truth to performances – and in this case the more experienced actor felt her counterpart didn't seem to be listening properly.

Watching them rehearse a scene, it became clear to me that the younger woman had all her weight on her heels; she appeared to be physically withdrawing from the dialogue. I spoke to her about it later and she told me she was nervous of acting with such a well-known and talented actor. I told her what I saw and that her fellow actors, however experienced, needed her to be very present in the scene – and that she could begin to achieve that by centring herself. With a little courage, she was able to do so – and in turn the two actors were able to produce wonderful, thrilling exchanges. This exercise will help you centre yourself too.

Exercise 2: Finding your centre of balance

Stand with your feet hip width apart and your knees unlocked. When you are comfortable, gently rock forward and back across your feet: not so far that you throw yourself completely off-balance, but just enough to be aware of the length of your feet; feel the toes, the balls and the heels as your weight shifts through your feet. Then, when you feel your weight is on the very centre of your feet, stop. You'll know when you are there because your feet will feel very comfortable.

How is that? Is your weight just a bit further forward than normal? Most of us tend to keep our weight on our heels; a slight pulling back from the world, which can be a protective instinct. Sometimes, like that young actress, we pull back to be polite or modest, or perhaps because we are afraid. But in physical terms, placing all your weight on your heels can put unnecessary pressure on your lower back and the back of your neck – these are the places that will tighten most to stop you from falling completely backwards. Remember, your aim is to have your weight balanced just in the middle of your feet, or 'centred'. When your weight is centred and balanced, you give your body more flexibility and potential for movement. You will also look different. Go back to the mirror and try the exercise there. I think you will see that when you are centred you don't look pushy or aggressive, reticent or withdrawn; you look more present, more engaged and more engaging.

Try making this change more subtly, shifting from your habitual stance to the new neutral position. You need to become familiar with it as you will probably have to find it quickly if you feel you are slipping back into your old, fixed, inflexible posture. You can also find the neutral position when you are standing in different ways; with your weight on one foot perhaps, or your feet close together. Try it. See if you can remain centred in those positions too, without pulling your weight back or locking your knees. When you get a sense of the balanced flexibility of centring your weight, you will be able to make it a new habit whatever you are doing. The neutral posture is not bland and it's not fixed. It is the position of freedom that is the starting point on your journey to charisma and better communication.

The neutral position isn't just about centring your weight through your legs and torso, however. You also need to consider how you carry your head. It always surprises me how many of us – including some actors – have our head fixed in an off-centre position; turned slightly to one side, or with the chin dropped or raised too high. This can create a bad impression: a person with their head a little to one side might seem a bit suspicious, as if they can't look a person straight in the eye; a chin always pulled down can look rather pompous or solemn. So, for actors and for you, having a neutral head position that looks the world in the eyes is a great starting point. It makes you look honest and candid.

Exercise 3: Centring your head

Stand again with your feet hip width apart and your knees unlocked. Then drop your chin down on to your chest. Feel how heavy your head is and enjoy the feeling of stretch through the muscles in your neck. Now, let your head float back up on to the top

---

of your neck, being careful not to let it drop back too far, with your chin too high. You have seven vertebrae in your neck; it is good to feel that they support your head. You should not feel that the back of your skull is pressing down on the top of your spine, nor should your chin be so high that you appear to be looking down your nose.

It's good to do this exercise in front of a mirror too, so that when you bring your head back up you can check the position. You should see that your head is level and that you are looking straight ahead. Then close your eyes for a moment to get in touch with the feeling of your head and neck in this position. When you open your eyes again, look around you so that you are moving your head from this centred position. Can you feel that your neck is moving freely? Now bring your head back to the new, level position.

Once you are familiar with centring your weight and freeing up your head position, you might like to try an exercise that actors do frequently in warm-ups, during rehearsals and sometimes in the wings before they go on stage. It brings them to the neutral posture by re-aligning the body all in one action. It also helps them to breathe deeply and it gets blood to the brain (and we can all do with that!). One actor I spoke to, Patrick Godfrey, has had a long career in theatre, film and television. He is now in his nineties, but says that he still always does this simple exercise in his warm-up.

Exercise 4: Finding a good posture

Standing with your feet hip width apart, let your head drop down on to your chest. Now, bend your knees a bit and then let your head lead the rest of your body downwards until you are bending over from the waist, as if you are rolling your body down. It doesn't matter if you aren't supple enough to touch your toes, you just need to go far enough to feel that your abdominal muscles are relaxed. If you can bend over far enough, they will be resting on the top of your thighs. Check that your neck is relaxed and that you are not holding your head up. While in this position, take a breath or two, then roll back up as if you are rebuilding your spine, vertebra by vertebra, until you finally bring your head up off your chest and into its centred position.

As you come up, make sure you don't let your weight fall back on to your heels again. Your aim should be to finish in your neutral, balanced position. Also be sure you aren't leading with your head or your shoulders, but instead allowing your spine to bring you up. Your shoulders should remain relaxed and dropped throughout. When you are upright again, check that your knees are soft and that your head is centred.

Finally, lift your shoulders up and then drop them, to check that they are in their most relaxed position. Tension in the shoulders is very common. It may be very visible or very slight, but either way it will affect how you use your voice. You can do this simple release at any time. I often suggest actors do it just before they go on stage.

Of course, none of us is standing all the time. You may also have to communicate informally and formally while seated. I once worked with a senior politician whose team were not happy with how he looked and sounded on television. Most of his interviews were conducted sitting down, but his desire to get his point across made him sit on the edge of his seat and push his energy forward. The resulting look belied his maturity and intellect; he looked like an eager young pup that wanted to have his head patted. It was clear to me that he needed to sit back comfortably in his chair and let the interviewer and the questions come to him. This starting posture did not make him seem laid-back, arrogant or laconic. He looked in control because he was in control of his body. Having a balanced, centred posture released his physical and vocal energy, and allowed him to move freely. When I next saw him on television, he gave a much better interview. He looked relaxed, his speech had more flow and he got his points across without being interrupted as frequently as in the past.

Like this overeager politician, you can become more charismatic while seated by considering your posture. Here, too, it helps to get into a neutral position. First, sit down in a comfortable upright chair, or use an office chair if you have one to hand. Your first step is to work out how you usually sit. Of course, this will vary from situation to situation – but for now, let's try to replicate how you would sit in a meeting, either in a group meeting or one to one. How do you hold yourself? Do you sit forward, showing your interest and energy? Do you jut your chin forward? Do you sink back to try to be invisible, or slouch to try to show how relaxed you are?

When we were working on your standing position, we focused on centring your weight on your feet. Centring is just as important when seated. In this case, the key lies not in your feet but in your 'sitting bones', the bones you feel in your bottom when your seated weight is placed evenly on them. Uncentred positions are when you either roll back off your sitting bones, and therefore round your spine and collapse the front of your body, or when you push your weight forward and your sitting bones are lifted off the chair as you arch the small of your back. This will cause tension in your lower back and the base of your neck. To avoid uncentring yourself, try to notice if you habitually roll back off your sitting bones, or tend to push your pelvis forward. Now, try shifting your weight and the position of your pelvis on to your sitting bones (you can still have your back against the chair if you wish). Can you feel your energy dropping down into your pelvis?

When you are sitting, your feet are still important, and you will find it very useful to have at least one foot flat on the ground. In theatre, we often talk about being 'grounded' or 'grounding' yourself. Indira Varma – an actor who has worked at the National Theatre and beyond, including on *Game of Thrones* and *Mission: Impossible* – is very familiar with this term. She describes it simply as 'feeling the ground beneath your feet'. It can be surprising how tension in our body pulls us up and away from the ground. To counteract that, being aware of your feet on the ground helps you to relax. Many actors find the very thought of being grounded can make them feel both relaxed and strong. So, when you are sitting and talking, sit on your sitting bones and have at least one foot flat on the ground. You may be most comfortable with your legs or ankles crossed, which is fine – but allow one foot to be flat on the floor.

MOVING FREELY

Olivier Award-winning actor Mark Gatiss has built his career playing characters with a distinctive physical presence. In 2015, he played Shpigelsky in *Three Days in the Country* – an adaptation of Turgenev's *A Month in the Country* – in the National Theatre's Lyttelton Theatre. Mark relished the physical humour of the role. There is a scene in which Shpigelsky attempts an amorous approach to another character but is hampered by his bad back. 'I knew at once what an amazing opportunity for physical comedy the "bad back" scene offered,' Mark says. 'With the director's encouragement, I changed the physicality all the time, trying to wring new laughs and surprise myself (without getting a hernia).' There is a limit, however. 'What I have learned, though, is to be careful. I played Robert Cecil in *Gunpowder*, and gave him a crooked neck,' he recalls. 'About a week into shooting, I thought "I wish I'd never started this!" I had referred back pain for weeks afterwards.'

Mark's experience shows how actors often need to be physically flexible to be able to respond effectively to the needs of their roles. The same is probably true for you, to some degree. By now, you will probably be feeling more comfortable when standing or seated. But whether you're an actor, or just someone who needs to 'perform' in day-to-day life, you don't just stay in one place; you will also want to move around at times.

Actors can struggle with movement almost as much as anyone. Having the skill to walk and talk at the same time on stage is something of a joke among theatre folk. How on earth can you focus on what you are feeling, what you are saying and who you are talking to, without bumping into the furniture? The truth is, even the most highly trained actors have physical mishaps from time to time. Most actors have bumped into or broken something, or fallen over on stage at some point. I remember watching Simon Russell Beale, playing Voltaire in a musical version of *Candide*, step backwards off the rim of the stage of the Olivier – the largest of the National's three theatres – into the lap of someone in the front row. No harm was done to either, fortunately. But not every such incident ends so happily. At the wonderful ancient Greek amphitheatre in Epidaurus, Alan Howard played Oedipus in a National Theatre production of Sophocles' *Oedipus Plays*. During the dress rehearsal, I watched him step sideways off a huge ramp and fall about fifteen feet. He was taken to hospital and returned in the evening to play the role with his arm in a sling – he'd broken his collarbone. In fact, the perils of moving on stage are so notorious that they have entered the realm of fable: there is an old theatrical adage that says if you fall over on a stage it means you will work there again.

How do you face the challenge of moving around freely when addressing an audience, then? Once again, before you think about speaking on the move, you need to be well-balanced and centred as you go. So let's work on that.

Allow yourself to go back to the way you normally stand, before you tried the neutral posture, and then take yourself for a walk. This is one of the first exercises actors do in drama school; they watch each other simply walking across the room. The ultimate objective is to learn about their *own* habits: after watching one another they walk again and think about how they move habitually themselves, and what it might reveal about them. As you are walking, think about your physical energy. How easy is it to walk? Do you get tired when walking? How do you move forward? Does your head lead the way? Your feet? Or maybe your chest or pelvis? Do you drive your energy forward or do you hang back in any way? Does your bottom get left behind or seem to pull you backwards?

Next, stop for a moment and find your standing neutral position, using the exercises we tried earlier. Begin walking again but try to maintain the neutral position: your body relaxed, your weight centred and your head upright. Your aim is to move with ease and flexibility in whatever direction you like. The best way to achieve this is to feel that you are moving from the centre of your whole body, and not leading with your head, your pelvis, your chest or your feet. It will also help you if you notice your relationship with the ground beneath your feet. Feel the pressure of your feet on the ground and how you roll through your feet as you move forward, and how your ankles are another moving part in the process. This should stop you from feeling fixed or stiff. As you become more aware of shifting from old patterns of tension, and discovering the advantages of being centred, you will find that a centred body is also an efficient body. It means you can breathe and therefore speak more easily, even when you are moving around.

However, there is one more element you need when you want to move with authority, and that is a sense of purpose. This is something actors are taught from early in their training. You might have sometimes seen actors doing a very strange, stilted walk across a stage: when they say, 'I'm leaving', for example, but don't have the force or forward momentum in their walk to make you believe they really will leave the scene. This happens when they are not moving within the reality of the drama; they are not 'in the moment', so the move lacks truth. The opposite of that is moving with a purpose: knowing exactly why they need to move, and then committing to it.

Generally, it is the director who suggests appropriate moves around the stage, which is called 'blocking'. But a good director will always allow actors to suggest moves that come from their instincts; from their understanding of what and why their character is speaking. Moving towards or away from another character will change their relationship with them: do they want to close the distance between them or lengthen it? Do they want to be more intimate or more controlling, perhaps? This can be useful when talking to an audience too. When Rory Kinnear played Hamlet at the National Theatre, he and director Nicholas Hytner decided he should stand right at the very front of the stage – 'downstage centre', very close to the audience – for his soliloquies. They made that choice so that he could talk to them as if they were his friends, to create a sense of intimacy.

So if you are giving a talk, a lecture or a presentation and decide that it would be a good idea to move around, you must have a really good reason to do so. Here, again, we can draw on the insights of Stanislavski. Identifying your character's 'intentions', moment by moment and scene by scene, is another modern acting technique that he developed. A character's intentions within a line or a scene are the things they wish to do or achieve. Having a clear sense of their character's intentions is one of the ways that actors create a reality for themselves within the story they are telling. If, when giving a presentation, you want your audience members to think about something in relation to their own work or experience, you might want to come out from behind your podium and move closer to them. If your intention is to make a broader point – a call to action or motivational statement aimed at everyone – you could move back so that you can have the whole room in your view. If you are using rhetorical questions, you could move towards different parts of the audience to ask them. Moving for the sake of it, on the other hand, will look peculiar. If your moves don't have an impulse that comes from your script or from your thoughts, you will look as awkward as our actor whose move wasn't connected to the truth of the scene.

The speed or pace of your moves must also be dictated by your purpose or intention. Do you want to appear calm or casual, moving in a relaxed way? Or do you want to change to a quicker pace, with a sense of spontaneity? Whatever you choose, linking movement to the point you are making will stop you from wandering aimlessly around the room or platform.

Of course, you won't want to be moving all the time. Simon Trinder – who has worked many times at the Royal Shakespeare Company and Shakespeare's Globe – helpfully suggests that when you run out of reasons to move, you 'find a physical resting position that makes you look and feel relaxed'. This is something he likes to find for every character he plays. It can become a default position or home base you can return to whenever you're not moving. For the actor, this would be connected to their character, the scene and their role in the play. But the principle applies in any situation where you need to communicate effectively. You could rest at a lectern, a table or chair. Your hands could be gently clasped in front of you or behind you; they could be holding something – a pen or a pointer. If you are seated for an interview, your hands could be resting in your lap, or on the arms of a chair. In every case, once you have made a decision about your resting position, then returning to it can be an anchor of sorts, one that brings a moment of rest for your mind and body. Adjoa Andoh told me about playing Condoleezza Rice in David Hare's play, *Stuff Happens*, at the National Theatre in 2016. She had a very big speech to deliver and was always pretty nervous about it, so she chose to rest against a table which was part of the set. This resting position helped her to remain in control.

Of course, crossing our 'stage' isn't the only way we move around when we are communicating. We also express ourselves with our hands. It can be surprisingly hard to keep your hands relaxed when you are in situations of heightened tension. This is true of actors too: many of them, especially when new to the profession, find they don't know what to do with their hands when they are speaking. Simon Trinder talks about the feeling of 'your hands being too big for your body', which happens when he doesn't know what his character is feeling. 'When you don't know what you want, your body doesn't know what to do.' This difficulty can lead to awkward, stiff hands and random gestures. One solution many actors and others reach for is 'pocket acting': keeping their hands in their pockets and sometimes gesticulating with them still there (not recommended!). If used thought-fully, pocket acting can be a useful solution to the hand problem, but it is easier for men than women, as male actors are more likely to be given trousers with pock-ets. Justine Mitchell, who has played many parts at the National Theatre, told me that she often goes out of her way to ask the production's costume designers to put pockets in her skirt, particularly when playing in period dramas. 'All women love skirts with pockets!' she says.

There is nothing wrong with putting your hands in your pockets or using a prop to anchor you – as long as it suits the situation and doesn't create tension. I recently worked on a play where one of the actors was playing a politician. In one scene he was at the centre of a public meeting. The actor was anxious about the scene and got into the habit of placing one hand in his pocket and raising his shoulder, thereby increasing his tension. I suggested he think of his hand in his pocket as a character choice; the politician wanting to look relaxed and at home. It then became a point of rest for the actor and the character, and so had a purpose. This logic applies to any sort of gesture, even when you're not acting. Your gesturing must have a purpose, to emphasise or draw attention to a specific point. And the gesture must be 'released', by letting the arm return to a relaxed position (perhaps simply hanging at your side). No one wants to see arms waving around repetitively; that is meaningless.

Often, no hand movement at all is very powerful; to just stand and speak can help you and your audience to focus on your argument, the words you are speaking. Nathalie Armin – an actor who has worked in theatre, film and television, including in *The Magpie Murders* and *Luther* – has been in several plays at the National Theatre and she admits that she is 'inclined to gesticulate wildly'. She says it can actually feel uncomfortable not moving, but that she tries to just keep her arms and hands still at times. 'It's perfectly fine to stand still and not gesture at all, and speak – don't do anything with them,' she says.

THE IMPORTANCE OF PREPARATION

When Christopher Saul was playing Egeon in *The Comedy of Errors* in 1996, the theatre director, Melly Still, led yoga sessions every morning. They were touring the play internationally and playing some big auditoriums, and Christopher felt under particular pressure because Egeon has a long speech that starts the play. The father of the twins who are at the heart of the story, Egeon tells in this speech how they were separated as babies in a storm at sea, when the ship they were on split in two, leaving one on each half. The speech wasn't just daunting because it opened the play, but also because of the staging: he had to sit in chains, cross-legged, centre stage, while the audience came in, from half an hour before the play began. Christopher found the yoga exercises to be particularly helpful as they were 'deep and energetic; stretching and disciplining every part of the actor, physically and mentally'. His routine, he told me, is what allowed his muscles to be flexible enough to endure this position for so long.

One need not undertake a full yoga exercise before every speech or interview. But physical preparation remains crucial when getting your body ready to perform. It came up time and again in my conversations with actors. As Tamsin Greig told me, 'We are physical beings and it's very important to stretch out, to warm up, to hydrate, to bring us into our "physical presence".' So once you've got used to the exercises in this section – but before you walk out on to your own stage, whatever that might be – make some time to prepare physically. It doesn't have to be a full workout; just a good stretch will release some tension and help you reset your body in preparation to own the room. Shaking out your limbs will also help. Then, before any speech, meeting or important conversation, remind yourself of a few of the simple steps we've explored in this chapter: lift and drop your shoulders to release shoulder and neck tension; make sure your weight is centred and your knees unlocked; and, if you are sitting, sit on your sitting bones and have at least one foot on the floor.

This physical preparation is important because, as we've seen in this chapter, the basis of all actor training is the body. Learning about their bodies and discovering a neutral, centred way to use them teaches actors who they are, and to have confidence in that knowledge. With a little time and thought, you can get to know your body well and discover how to use it efficiently, effectively and, above all, authentically.

CHAPTER 2

YOUR VOICE

The real meat of my work is carried out during a play's four- to six-week rehearsal period. During this time, I watch rehearsals to find out what the particular vocal demands on the actors are, monitor how they are using their voices, and work with them individually.

One of the most challenging situations is when a leading actor is inexperienced or out of practice and their part is so large that I can't get enough time with them on their own. This is particularly likely when the actor is young, and on stage all or almost all the time. One such play was *The Curious Incident of the Dog in the Night-Time*, one of the National Theatre's biggest hits of recent years. While Simon Stephens' play of Mark Haddon's book has now been put on all over the world, it was originally performed in our smallest theatre, the Dorfman, in 2012, under the direction of Marianne Elliott. Christopher, the leading character, is a highly intelligent young man and, although it is never stated in the book or the play, he appears to be autistic. It is a difficult role. Because of the age of the character, the actor cast is always young (it is sometimes their first job) and Christopher is on stage all the time.

What's more, the role is very physically and vocally demanding. The story is partly told through movement, often of a spectacularly expressive and inventive kind – at times, it is almost gymnastic. So all the actors must undergo a full physical training routine during rehearsals, which they then keep up throughout the run of the show. In addition, Christopher uses strong expressive noises when he can't articulate his feelings. All of this means the role can take its toll on the actor's body and voice. Ideally, he would begin voice work with me or one of my team before rehearsals begin, but this isn't always possible. Once rehearsals are under way, it is practically impossible for him to have time away from the rehearsal room with the voice coach, and we have to wait until the play has opened before we can give proper voice training to support the actor.

These are unusual demands to be placed upon a voice, but the principles behind the work done with these actors are the same for everyone who wants to keep their voice strong, healthy, and most importantly, expressive. Whether you have hundreds of sessions with a voice coach, or just a couple; whether you have months to prepare, or just a few hours now and again; and even if you are working alone, you will be drawing on the same basic tools that I introduce in this chapter.

BREATHING

I sometimes tell actors that I'm going to have 'don't forget to breathe' tattooed on my forehead, because I say it so often. You may not believe that we can stop breathing, but in real life, when we listen and think, we often suspend our breath. When we are relaxed, we naturally take in a nice breath before we speak. But if we aren't relaxed – when we are, say, in a high-stakes meeting, or about to start an important presentation – it is common for us not to breathe in. This breath-holding means we are holding tension in the mouth, the jaw, the throat and the shoulders.

This is something that even the most experienced actors continue to grapple with. Nathalie Armin admits that sometimes she is so nervous on stage, usually in the first few performances of a play, that her breathing becomes very shallow, she gets light-headed and thinks she's about to faint. Then, because of the shallow breathing, her voice becomes very underpowered and thin. She recalled a conversation we had about this when we were working together on an American play at the National Theatre in

2015, called *The Motherfucker with the Hat*, by Stephen Adly Guirgis. My advice had been very simple: I told her to just stop and breathe. So, now when she gets very scared on stage and loses control of her voice, she reminds herself: 'Just breathe and you'll get the right tone again.' It is a simple piece of advice, and I give it frequently.

How you breathe will affect your listeners too. Peter Forbes illustrated this when telling me about his experience at Shakespeare's Globe Theatre. The theatre is a fine replica of an Elizabethan playhouse, situated on the South Bank of the river Thames in London. At the ground level, in front of the stage, are 'the groundlings' – members of the audience who stand to watch – and it is a common phenomenon for some of those to faint during performances. Peter wondered whether the problem wasn't the heat, but that so many members of the audience become deeply involved in what is happening on the stage. He says, 'The actors were always being told to remember to breathe: if you don't breathe, they won't breathe.' When we listen to people speaking, including actors in a play, we have a tendency to mirror how they are behaving, especially their breathing.

Every actor I spoke to for this book mentioned breath in some capacity. When they talked about conquering stage fright, they mentioned breath. When they emphasised preparing for a role and warming up, they mentioned breath. When they told me how they used their scripts, they mentioned breath. And, of course, when we spoke about voice, they mentioned breath. Good breathing matters, and it matters on several levels: it fuels your voice for effective speech; it feeds your brain so you can think clearly; it can help you control your nerves; and it also contributes to relaxation. As the Olivier Award-winning actor Deborah Findlay summarises it, 'Breathing is just very important; as soon as you take a deep breath, everything relaxes.' Danny Sapani said something similar: 'Finding my centre and being able to breathe into my gut in turn relaxes my shoulders and makes me feel very present, very grounded.'

So here, I'm going to show you how to breathe into your gut – your abdomen – and I'm going to share with you some of the exercises I use with actors to achieve that. To be sure you have some knowledge to back up the exercises, I'm first going to explain how breathing works.

Let's start by picturing the lungs and ribcage. The lungs are, of course, contained in the chest, beneath the ribcage, and they are pear-shaped: bigger at the bottom than the top. Therefore, you can get more air into the bottom of your lungs than the top. The ribcage is made up of twelve pairs of ribs. The top seven pairs are attached to the spine at the back and the breastbone at the front. The lower five pairs are attached to the spine at the back but are not attached directly to the breastbone at the front. This means the ribs at the bottom of the ribcage move most easily. As a result, you breathe more effectively if you learn to breathe deeply into the bottom, larger part of your lungs. If you take a big breath and feel your upper chest and shoulders rise, you are breathing mainly into the top of your lungs. That is what is called shallow breathing. It might feel like a big breath, but it's not a deep one, or a useful breath to speak with. It may feel as if you've taken in a lot of air, but that's because you are trying to fill the smallest parts of your lungs.

Attached all the way around the bottom of the ribcage is the diaphragm. This is a flexible, dome-shaped sheet of muscle that divides the body in half; it forms the floor of the chest and the ceiling of the abdomen. As you breathe in, the centre of your diaphragm lowers and your ribs widen. This gives more space in your chest for your lungs to fill with air. If you place your fingers just below the bottom of your breastbone, you will feel a little movement in your muscles and stomach as the diaphragm moves down when you breathe in. It is very important that you recognise this movement because it is vital for the proper filling of your lungs. Everything beneath the diaphragm has to be able to move as the diaphragm moves. If the diaphragm can't move down fully, the air can't be drawn down into the lower part of the lungs and will only fill the upper, smaller sections; as you will see later, this action can restrict the freedom of your larynx.

So how can we make sure we're breathing in a way that will help us perform? That's the focus of the exercises in this section. Your overall goal is to learn to breathe into the abdomen. When the actors I interviewed for this book talked about breathing, they discussed the feeling of breathing deep into their body, and the movement they feel internally and externally in the muscles of their abdomen when they do so. We describe this as breathing to and speaking from the belly, or the tummy.

The million-dollar question when it comes to voice and breath is this: Do you hold your abdominal muscles tight? Lots of us do so a lot of the time, and there are many reasons why. One of them is the desire for physical strength and fitness – nothing wrong in that – but it brings with it an emphasis on core strength, and sports coaches will often encourage you to hold your abdominal muscles tight all the time. The Christophers in *The Curious Incident* came up against this problem. Because of the extreme physicality of the role, they were taught to strengthen their core, but in order to manage their voices well, they had to learn when to release their abdominal muscles for speech. Another reason many of us hold these muscles tight is aesthetic. We are taught that a flat or muscular abdomen is extremely attractive. This is particularly the case for young actors who are often under pressure to be seen as perfect specimens of humanity. But if you tighten your abdominal muscles, you will never breathe in fully and your voice will be high and shallow, and you will never fully release its power. Fulfilling the potential of your voice depends on fulfilling the potential of your breath – and that means releasing your abdomen.

So to begin with, let's see if you can feel your breath moving into the lower part of your lungs. Sit in an upright chair, with your feet placed flat on the ground. It is useful to try out good breathing when you are sitting down as you are unlikely to hold your stomach in tight when sitting. It doesn't matter if your back is against the back of the chair; just make sure you are comfortably upright and sitting on your sitting bones, as we practised in the last chapter, not slouching or pushing forward. Now, see if you can become aware of the movement of your ribs as you breathe. Can you feel the lower part of your ribcage moving slightly out and in at the front of your body? Maybe you can also feel a bit of movement in the back of your ribcage and at the sides? Next, try taking a big breath. Does the air go straight into your upper chest? Try again and see if you can direct it into the lower part of your lungs and ribcage. When you can feel the pressure below your waist as your diaphragm moves downwards, that is the feeling of breathing into your abdomen.

This is the kind of breathing that will most 'support' your voice, and that will quickly get you relaxed and ready to speak. However, to develop a habit that will serve you when you are stepping up a gear and performing to an audience, here are some exercises you can practise – all of which I often do with actors in their warm-ups.

The first step to prepare your body for deep, low breathing is stretching. Sometimes I think we should be like cats and whenever we have the impulse to stretch, do so. All the actors I spoke to about their warm-ups said they begin with some sort of stretching, so that their ribcage and shoulder joints can be free enough to allow for more breath. Stretching releases tension, increases blood flow to your muscles, and increases the flexibility of your ribcage and shoulder joints. This simple exercise will help you do all three.

Exercise 1: A three-way rib stretch

Stand with your feet a bit wider apart than your hips and with your weight centred. Lift your right arm up above your head with your fingers pointed to the ceiling. Try to keep your shoulders relaxed.

Next, drop your right hand on to your head, then bend your knees a little and lean over to the left side. You should now feel a stretch in the right side of your ribcage. Wrap your other arm around the front of your body until you can place your left hand on the stretched right side. Take a couple of breaths and see if you can feel the stretched side of your ribs move under your hand as you breathe. Finally, come back up to centre and drop your arms. Take a breath and see how free that side of your body feels. Repeat on the other side.

Now, drop your head on to your chest, bend your knees a little and then roll down through your spine until you are bending over from the bottom of your ribs at the back – though not quite as far over as you rolled down in the posture exercise on page 31. Let your arms hang loose, or, if this is uncomfortable, rest your hands or your forearms on your thighs but be sure to keep your back rounded. Take a couple of big breaths and notice your abdomen moving towards your thighs. Also be aware of the movement of your ribs in your lower back as you breathe in.

Roll up again, until you are poised, with your head level. Your instinct may be to pull your abdominal muscles in as you come up. Remember, in order to breathe properly, you need to release them.

Once you've finished this exercise, take a moment to notice your breathing again. Can you feel the movement in your abdomen and your lower ribs? Can you direct your breath there? Can you enjoy the feeling of breathing down into your abdomen with your abdominal muscles relaxed? When Patrick Godfrey and I were discussing vocal projection he said, 'Don't be afraid to put your stomach out.' You should learn to love that feeling. I always tell actors that I'm teaching them to own the natural release of their abdominal muscles. I tell them that my stomach isn't fat, it's released!

Now that you've stretched out your upper body around your ribcage, you can do a simple breathing exercise that actors do in every voice warm-up. It is quite aerobic: it gets you breathing deeply and floods your body with oxygen. It also helps you to control both your breath and your nerves. You will find it useful when you are preparing for an important speech, but if you do it regularly, you will find you increase the capacity of your breath, and that when you speak, your voice will sound fuller.

Exercise 2: A breathing exercise for control and increased capacity

You can do this exercise sitting comfortably upright or standing in your neutral position. Take a deep breath down into your abdomen and your lower ribs. Make sure that your shoulders and upper chest remain relaxed.

Release the breath on a long 'Sssssss' until you run out of breath – but not going so far that you tighten your throat to try to squeeze out more air. Then let the breath come in again and release a second long 'Sssss'. Breathe in again and release a third long 'Sssss'. Each time, try to release your breath in a long, slow, steady stream.

How does that feel? As you release your breath, notice that you can control the flow by following the movement of your ribs as they move slowly down and inwards. If your main focus is on your lower ribs, around your waist, you should be able to feel that your abdominal muscles stay quite stable until towards the end of your breath. Then there comes a moment when you will feel them become involved. It is this stability of your abdominal muscles that supports the steady release of your breath. If you can become very familiar with this feeling, it will be the support for your voice when you speak – the subject to which we now turn.

A RESONANT VOICE

The sound of our voice is made by vibrating air that we breathe out of our lungs. The vibrations happen in the vocal folds in the throat. Voice is simply vibrating air.

We create these vibrations when we speak, sing, laugh, cry, sneeze, cough or moan. The vocal folds are now no longer called the vocal cords, as that word implies that they are single strands, like the strings of a guitar. In fact, they are two bands of muscular tissue which span the middle of three cartilages, just behind your Adam's apple. These cartilages, sitting one on top of the other, form the larynx. If you place a finger on your Adam's apple and hum, you will feel the vibrations.

Above the vocal folds are three spaces that amplify the sound made by your vocal folds. The first of these is just above the vocal folds, in your larynx. The second is your mouth. And the third are your nasal sinuses, the spaces at the top of your nose and in your skull between your eyes. The amplifying spaces in your mouth and throat are flexible, but they are also very badly affected by tension – and tension here will make it more difficult for you to speak clearly and loudly.

You can experiment with the effects of tension. Tighten your shoulders a little. Can you feel that in your throat? Bite your back teeth together. Can you feel that in your throat? If you tighten the corners of your mouth, you will also feel a corresponding tightening in your throat. This may not be familiar to you but some people do it habitually. It might happen when you are trying to look interested or happy and it can become fixed – something I call 'the pleasing face'. In these moments, tension in the face can become a type of mask, interfering with the easy release of your voice. The first step towards finding your authentic voice, then, is again about relaxation, this time of the face and throat. Releasing this tension will free up the spaces that amplify your voice, ensuring that it will resonate fully and the range of notes you use will increase. This will then allow your voice to be more expressive.

It's time to go back to the mirror. This time, have a good look at your face. Even when it is just you looking, do you appear relaxed? Do you bite your back teeth together? Do you frown or do you have a permanent smile? Any of these can be caused by tension and anxiety. But there are some simple exercises you can use to help you release these facial tensions. You can use them at any point, but they are particularly good preparation for any big presentation, performance or meeting.

A really effective way to stretch out and release the muscles of your face, jaw and throat is simply to yawn. If you can't yawn at will, try yawning with your mouth closed, as if you are stifling a yawn. That is usually easier and gives your throat a really big stretch. Massage can help, too. In front of your ears, on both sides of your face, are the muscles that attach your top jaw, which is your cheekbone, to your bottom jaw. Take your fingertips into this place and gently massage. Releasing tension here can release tension in the back of your mouth, your neck and your chest, because the muscles in this area are all linked. Now extend the massage to other parts of your face and neck: your hairline, your forehead, your cheeks and your jawline; between your eyes, around your mouth. Massage around your ears to the back of your neck, and down on to your shoulders too. You can finally massage your throat by gently stroking down your larynx with the finger and thumb of one hand. Use just a little pressure. Do you feel it release the back of your throat?

Now that you've released and relaxed your face and throat, you can focus on the vibrations of your voice: its resonance. In theatre voice training, to develop the resonance of our voices, we use humming. When you hum you keep your mouth shut, which means you can feel your voice strongly vibrating through the spaces, muscles and bones of your body. This is useful, as when you apply this resonance to words, you will have a sense of the voice coming from your whole body before sending it out into the world. Many actors use humming in their warm-up routines and I always use it in the warm-ups I lead. As Niamh Cusack, who has played many leading roles at the National Theatre as well as on film and TV, told me, 'I do a bit of breathing lying on the floor: stretching my tongue and face then humming. Then I get up to standing and continue humming, up and down.'

Exercise 3: Humming for resonance

You can do this exercise standing or sitting in your centred position. Breathe gently down into your abdomen, then begin to hum on any comfortable note. Breathe when you need to, and then hum on different notes. As you hum, be sure to keep the spaces in your mouth and throat relaxed so that the sound has room to resonate. Don't press your lips together as this will reduce the space in your mouth and cause tension. You will probably feel the vibrations on your lips and in your nose – enjoy those.

Focusing on vibrations around the mouth and nose has traditionally been a way of bringing your voice forward, so that it readily comes out of your mouth. When we focus the voice into different parts of our face and body, we call this 'placing the resonance' or 'placing your voice'. This is done purely using the imagination; imagining the vibrations of your voice travelling to these different places. Singers do it too as part of the process of projecting their voices, and it also helps them to improve the quality and pitch of each note they sing.

It might seem odd to use the imagination to assist with something as practical as a voice warm-up. But in fact, the imagination is very important to voice work, because we can't see or touch our voice. Actors depend on lively imaginations to create their characters, so they are used to using their imagination when it comes to voice work. You will see how useful it is too; the voice really does respond well to the imagination. Imagine that your lungs go right down into your abdomen as you breathe in – try it now as you read this. Then try the humming again and see if you can create a feeling of the resonance of your voice coming from there too. Working with your imagination allows you to quickly tune in to breathing and speaking from your abdomen. Hopefully, with enough practice, this is the way you will always speak; it will become instinctive.

Strangely, this very act of thinking the voice into different parts of your body has a major impact on how it sounds to your audience. Peter Forbes told me a story that demonstrated this point, from his experience when playing Buddy in Dominic Cooke's production of Stephen Sondheim's musical *Follies* at the National Theatre in 2017 and 2019. He spoke of a moment in one of his songs called 'The Right Girl', where the musical director, Nicholas Skilbeck, wanted him to sing very quietly. Peter was concerned about audibility but was reassured by Nicholas that his radio microphone and the sound design would support his voice fully and he would still be heard, despite the volume of the orchestra. 'My focus wasn't so much on volume or how much sound I was putting out,' Peter told me. 'Just how focused the resonance of it was – even when it was almost whispering.' He told me that he focuses the resonance of his voice forward in his mouth, and by so doing he feels that he can communicate his thoughts through sound; in this case, through the words of the song.

If you concentrate and have begun to develop an awareness of sensations in your body, you will realise you can place the resonance of your voice anywhere around it. If you touch your face, your head, your neck or your chest as you hum, you will probably be able to feel the vibrations as they travel into the bones that are near the surface. If you touch lower in your body, where the bones are covered by more muscle, you might not feel the vibrations travelling into your hands. However, if you focus or *think* the resonance of your voice to those lower places – your abdomen, your back or even your legs and feet – you may have a sense on the inside that your vibrating voice is travelling right through you. If you are able to do this, you will hear that your voice is enriched.

As you start playing with the resonance of your voice, try to have some fun with your body and your voice. Really let it go. Lots of actors' exercises are playful; they find that breaking away from the inhibition of adult life, even in a small way, can be liberating for the voice and the imagination. So, to help you to feel the vibrations right through your body, try shaking out your arms and legs as you hum. Or bounce up and down a bit. Can you feel vibrating sound being released right through you? I'm sure you will hear the sound change; don't worry if your voice wobbles a bit. You could also try shaking your spine and your behind ('twerking' is the term, I believe). Or try lots of different notes, sliding your voice up and down and all around. Hum some tunes with a sense of the different parts of the melodies resonating in different parts of your body, but make sure you don't tighten up in your face, jaw or throat as you go for higher notes. It doesn't matter if you aren't making beautiful music; your aim is to explore the range of your voice so that it can eventually be more expressive when you speak.

Once you have really got going with humming, focus the resonance back on to your lips. Now play with opening and closing your mouth to let your voice out and then catching it on the lips again. The sound you will make is 'hm, m, m, m, m, m' etc., like a baby playing with their voice and ending up saying 'mama'. Then try releasing different vowels sounds: 'me, may, mah' and 'moo, moh, maw'. Then release different resonant words beginning with 'm': 'Many men making much money in the moonshine'. Can you feel the glorious buzz of that? Try some other words, counting for example. Can you retain that resonance? If so, you are now well on the way to having a fully resonant speaking voice.

VOCAL EXPRESSIVENESS

So far in this section, you've learned to relax your face and throat muscles and to develop a more resonant sound. Now you can learn to make use of the full range and expression of your voice.

The key, once again, is breathing. If you neglect your easy, deep breathing to support your voice, your throat will eventually try to push out some sound. To do that the muscles of your throat will contract, making the amplifying spaces smaller, so your voice will lack the resonance it needs to be expressive. When the amplifying spaces close down, so does the range of your voice. It becomes more monotone.

This lack of breath support can lead to what I call a creaky voice; a sound that is lacking in energy and creates a tone that might be so dominant it distracts the listener from what the speaker is saying. Without enough breath, the vocal folds won't vibrate effectively, and the sound cannot be properly resonant. This sound can be a choice, however, and there are reasons for people choosing to speak in this way. Sometimes people creak when they sit only in the lower notes of their voice, wanting to have a deeper voice than their natural one; they perhaps feel that deeper voices indicate maturity, authority and gravitas. Sometimes people sit in the lower register of their voice when they want to convey some particularly serious information, or to show that they take something seriously. Whatever the reason, if the creak happens it is because they are trying to use notes they do not really have or have not developed.

If this is something you recognise in your own voice, you can change that and get the best quality of voice by learning to free up your body, your breath and your resonance. When you speak without enough breath, or without enough space in your vocal tract for resonance, your listeners end up listening to *how* you speak and not to *what* you are speaking. It can be both frustrating and irritating for your audience and it certainly doesn't present confidence. As Nathalie Armin puts it, 'When I hear people who deliver everything on one level . . . I can't understand it. On film it's bad enough but on stage, it's unbearable.'

If you are concerned that your voice is creaky or rather monotone – and consequentially less expressive – here is an exercise to help you change that.

Exercise 4: To gain more expression and variety in your speaking voice

Standing or sitting comfortably and centred, be sure to breathe from your abdomen. You are going to count up from one. Start by speaking 'one' at the lowest note you can easily speak.

Then speak 'two' in the highest note you can easily speak. That might be a 'head note', as we call the notes that tenors or sopranos can use for singing. When these notes are used by a person without a trained singing voice, I call that range of notes your 'child's voice'. Continue in this manner: speaking 'three' on the low note, then 'four' on the high note, and so on, all the way to ten.

Once you've finished, go back to the beginning – but this time count to ten normally.

Can you hear that having used a wide range of notes in the exercise, your voice sounds more expressive when you speak normally again? This is because you will now be naturally using more vocal range.

You should now try the same exercise on a piece of text. It could be helpful to use something that you are working on but a passage from a novel or a newspaper, or a piece of poetry would be fine. When using this text, instead of changing from low to high on single words, you change on every syllable. It will sound very silly, and that is fine too.

I'll demonstrate with a line from Shakespeare's Sonnet 18:

```
        I       pare      to      sum      day?
Shall     com       thee     a      mer's

        art      love     and      tem      ate.
Thou     more      ly      more     per
```

Now speak it again normally:

Shall I compare thee to a summer's day?
Thou art more lovely and more temperate.

I learned this exercise from Patsy Rodenburg, a brilliant voice teacher and former Head of Voice at the National Theatre. It's an exercise we often use for actors preparing their voices for big theatres. In everyday life, in normal conversations, we probably only use the lower half of our vocal range. But if you try to speak in a big room using just that low range, you will find it hard work. The voice will have to push for volume, and your range of expression will be limited.

That's why we train our actors to become familiar with speaking from the centre of their range. This area has more energy and gives easy access to the whole range of the voice and is therefore naturally expressive. It makes speaking with more volume effortless.

SPEAKING WITH CLARITY

When I spoke to Tamsin Greig, I told her that I felt one of her defining characteristics as an actor was her clarity: of thought, of movement and above all of speech. She surprised me by telling me that being heard clearly in the theatre is something that she has really had to work at. She says there was a time when she wasn't heard clearly, 'because I hadn't brought in all of the elements that are necessary to create that clarity.'

This difficulty with clarity had been brought home to Tamsin when she returned to the stage after a decade away. She had had a ten-year break from theatre when her children were small. When she returned, she was not 'reading a few poems above a pub in a lunchtime', but performing at the Royal Shakespeare Company in two plays: Beatrice in *Much Ado About Nothing* and Constance in *King John*.

It was a daunting experience. She originally thought the idea was 'madness, madness!' – but was eventually persuaded to take the job by her husband and her agent. If that weren't intimidating enough, during previews of the first production, *Much Ado*, her husband and the play's director, Marianne Elliott, both told her she couldn't be heard by the whole theatre. The experience shook her, Tamsin tells me. She thought she had been shouting, but they told her that she was probably only reaching the front rows. She said she now recognises that she 'wasn't under-standing the physical nature of getting her voice into the whole auditorium'.

What had helped her, she tells me, was realising that Shakespeare is 'presenting a piece of art, like a painting'. That requires a different approach to day-to-day speech: 'It's not the natural order, and it takes a long time to put it all into focus and present an argument with such clar-ity and dexterity.' Similarly, she felt, 'it is like a work of art to think well and to project well. To take our intention and allow it to go on a physical, metaphorical and psycho-logical journey.'

Tamsin is describing something very fundamental in the acting process; something that many young actors find almost impossible to deal with, at least when they first take on roles in big theatres. As they often discover when practising in the Olivier Theatre, what feels unnaturally precise and loud to them on stage sounds perfectly natural and easy to follow from the auditorium. You may not be speaking in a big theatre but whenever you want to hold the attention of a group, it is important to energise your articulation so that everyone can hear you easily. That is why in this section I am going to teach you how to prepare your mouth and your tongue for clarity of speech. We will explore how to make the step from the full, free, expressive sound that we developed in the last section to clear speech, whatever environment you are speaking in. Once again, you will need to look at your habits – and this time, the way you habitually use your mouth, face and jaw when you speak.

To become aware of these, you should go back to the mirror and this time try saying something and watch how you use your mouth, face and jaw. Consider how much or how little you move your mouth when you speak. If someone needed to lip-read what you are saying, how easy would that be? You might be surprised at how little you move your mouth, but the more energy you have in your mouth movements, the more energy you will have in your words. If you are brave enough, I recommend that you video yourself speaking or reading. Use something you might speak or read at work, or even record a conversation with someone, and have a go both sitting and standing – in your best neutral positions of course. (If you do record yourself, remember that the sound you hear from the recording element on your phone doesn't give you the full range of resonance that we hear in real life, so don't judge yourself harshly on the tone of voice you hear.)

Your goal is to speak with more energy in your articulators – the muscles that shape your words – so that you can share your thoughts more expressively and, when necessary, share them easily with a large group of people. Key to this are the spaces in your face and throat that amplify your voice; when they are open and flexible, they allow you to speak more clearly and fluently. So, let's begin the next stage of your work by considering the space inside your mouth and the movement of your tongue. Take a moment or two to think about and explore the inside of your mouth. Start by opening it wide and having a look inside through the mirror. Have a good look at your tongue. It's not just the bit you can stick outside your mouth, it goes right down inside your throat at the back. It is attached to the top of your larynx at the top of your throat, so it can have an influence on the amplifier in your throat, and on your vocal folds.

Next, look at the roof of your mouth. See that it has ridges on the hard palate near your teeth, then it arches up in the centre. At the back, it has a drop of flesh hanging down. That's your uvula and it is the very back of your palate. Next, slowly draw the tip of your tongue over your palate from front to back: starting from behind your top teeth, slide your tongue back over the ridges and up into the arch. Go back even further and you will feel that the palate right at the back is softer. This is your soft palate and it is the doorway to the back of your nose; the door to your nasal amplifiers. It is flexible and movable. In fact, it moves quite a lot as you make different speech sounds. Exploring the inside of your mouth with your tongue should make you realise how flexible your tongue is, and how dexterously it can move. If you can optimise this dexterity, you will be able to speak more clearly.

You can do this by learning to loosen and exercise your tongue. The exercises that follow are a staple of the pre-performance voice warm-ups that I lead. For many actors, they are the most important exercises because they are about being able to speak clearly and fluently.

Exercise 5: For lingual dexterity

Move your tongue all around your mouth. Push it into every corner, including your teeth. (Maybe you will find some tasty morsel left over from your last meal or snack.)

Open your mouth and see how much movement you can make with your tongue. Can you do tongue gymnastics? Give it a good workout.

If you can, make a rolled 'R' sound, moving your voice up and down as you roll the 'R'. This really energises the muscles at the tip of the tongue, which you use for many consonant sounds. It is very important for clear speech.

The most important element in getting the best movement out of your tongue when you speak is to have enough space in your mouth. But how, in practice, can we increase the amount of space in our mouths when we speak? One classic exercise is to practise with a 'bone prop', which was widely used in acting schools through the twentieth century. In those days, the prop was a small piece of bone, about 10cm in length, with a piece of string tied through it. The actor would lightly hold the bone between their front teeth in order to keep some space in their mouth – the string was there to make sure they didn't swallow it. They would then practise consonant sequences, tongue twisters or their speeches, with the bone prop between their teeth. Patrick Godfrey tells me that at Central School of Speech and Drama, where he trained in the 1950s, this was a favoured method; to this day he still uses it at every warm-up, improvising a bone prop of his own from something plastic. He explains that it means 'knowing you are going to get around the words of a Shakespeare speech'. Here is my own version of the bone prop.

Exercise 6: The twenty-first-century bone prop

Take a plastic bottle cap. It could be the top of a milk bottle or water bottle. Place it in its flat position, between your back teeth on one side of your mouth, and hold it in place without biting down on it too hard. Now try speaking or reading something aloud as you hold the cap between your back teeth.

It won't be very easy to speak but you should try to do so as clearly as possible. When you have spoken or read several sentences, take the cap out and speak the same thing again. Does it feel easier to speak than normal? Can you feel how flexible your tongue feels and how clearly you are making consonant sounds? That's because you have found more space in your mouth. The more you practise speaking with the bottle top in your mouth, the more you will get used to the space and enjoy speaking clearly.

When you are looking at yourself speaking, take particular note of your mouth movements. Try putting a bit more energy on to your lips when you speak words using m, b, p, w, o, oo, oh, ou. It shouldn't be so much movement that you feel that you are 'mugging', as we say in theatre – that is, overdoing your facial expressions. But bear in mind that if you don't move your mouth enough habitually, making more movement can feel unnatural at first. As always, you will have to practise and find a good balance, where you are increasing the energy of your articulators – the mouth, the tongue and the jaw – while still speaking authentically.

So far, we've explored three ways to enhance the clarity of your speech: first, by learning to move your tongue with greater dexterity; second, by increasing the amount of space in your mouth; and third, by moving your mouth more while speaking. Our final area of focus is just as important: emphasising the clear pronunciation of consonants made with your tongue.

Actors know that to be properly heard and understood in a big theatre, they have to be clear and energetic with all consonant sounds. That's why during the rehearsals of every new production to be performed in the National's two bigger theatres, the Olivier and Lyttelton, I would take the company of actors into the empty theatre so that they could try out their voices and discover or remind themselves what they need to do to be heard easily. I would lead a vocal warm-up and then they would take it in turns to speak something from the stage while the rest of the cast sat in or moved around the auditorium to see how well they could hear each other from different seats. Depending on how far they were into rehearsals, they might try speeches or scenes from the play, or they might speak something else they knew. The first thing the actors who were listening noticed was that they had to be very clear and precise with consonants. When the consonants are too soft, it can be really hard to engage with the actor and what they are saying.

So if you want to communicate effectively, you need to pronounce consonant sounds clearly and with energy. Here is an exercise that helps.

Exercise 7: Consonant exercises

For the tip of the tongue

With a relaxed jaw, take a breath and repeat the following sequence. Begin carefully, making sure every sound is shaped well. Then, gradually speed up. Can you maintain the precision of the sounds?

Start with T: *tee, tay, tah, too, toe, taw.*
Then repeat with D: *dee, day, dah, doo, doh, daw.*
Then with L: *lee, lay, lah, loo, loh, law.*
Then with N: *nee, nay, nah, noo, noh, naw.*
Then with S: *see, say, sah, soo, soh, saw.*

For the back of the tongue

Take a breath and make the following K sounds:
kee, kay, kah, koo, koh, kaw.

Then repeat with G sounds (using a hard g): *gee, gay, gah, goo, goh, gaw.*

For the sides of the tongue

Take a breath and say: *yee, yay, yah, yoo, yoh, yaw.*

For the lips

Take a breath and say: *bee, bay, bah, boo, boh, baw.*
Repeat with P: *pee, pay, pah, poo, poh, paw.*

Our final exercise is a way to put together everything we've covered in this section. Tongue twisters are useful because they increase the mobility of the tongue and mouth; I nearly always use them at the end of the actors' warm-up. But for tongue twisters to be effective, you have to practise them with a free jaw and space in your mouth. This will allow your tongue to move freely, and for the sound of your voice to ring out.

Exercise 8: Some tongue twisters

- A bigger ball bounces better, the biggest ball bounces best.
- A better bit of butter, a better bit of butter.
- The train rattled through the tunnel and trundled into the station.

- David dug a deeper ditch than Donald with his digger.
- A creepy, crawly creature like a caterpillar can't escape the clutches of a cat.
- Pretty Penelope, pretty Penelope, pretty Penelope.
- The car crash was a catastrophe.

(For extra dexterity, you could practise these articulation exercises and tongue twisters with your bottle top between your back teeth; that will really give your tongue and lips a good workout!)

When you are preparing to speak at an important occasion, whether it is just to one person or a whole auditorium, these mouth and tongue exercises should be an important part of your warm-up. It can be difficult to have a quiet, private moment if you are a guest speaker or work in a busy office – so if you have to, you can do some of them silently in the privacy of a toilet cubicle, just so long as you get some space in your mouth and get your tongue exercised. But wherever you do them, they will make an enormous difference to the way you can use your voice – helping you release tension in your face and jaw and energise your tongue.

ACCENT AND CLARITY

When I talk about 'clarity', some people think I am suggesting that everybody should speak in the same, southern English accent. I mean nothing of the sort. Clarity of voice is achievable in any accent and in any language, and none of the exercises I am showing you mean that you have to change your original accent.

In theatre, we represent the whole of humanity and our actors learn to speak clearly in many different accents. Our aim is always inclusivity; we want to share the stories we tell with everyone, and variety of accent is one of the joys of speech. Whether you are explaining the findings of your research, giving a speech, or simply recounting an anecdote, you will want to share your stories with your authentic accent.

The goal of all the work we have done in this chapter is not to change your style of speech but to ensure that everyone who listens to you hears what you are saying and enjoys listening to you. That doesn't mean you won't hear changes. As you open up your vocal range and become more expressive, the tune of your accent comes more into play. The tune of an accent is often one of its distinguishing characteristics and when a speaker's voice is open, free and energised it can be a great communication tool.

So don't be afraid that by working on your voice you will lose your authentic accent. Your accent is part of your authenticity. When you are centred and your voice is resonant and supported by breath that comes from deep within you, your listeners hear that as being authentic to you, to sounding like you. But you do have to work at it. As Adjoa Andoh puts it, 'Your voice is just a muscle. If you don't warm it up and you don't exercise it enough, you will fuck it!'

PART II
AUTHORITY

CHAPTER 3

BEING IN CONTROL

When a young actor is given their first lead role, one of the many challenges they face is to find within themselves the authority to lead the company. This can be quite a struggle, and I am often called upon to work closely with the actor to help them meet the challenge. Being one of 'the company' – the members of the cast without a leading role – where your only responsibility is playing your character truthfully, and supporting everyone else, can be comfortable. When you find yourself in a lead role, things change. Now, both company and audience need to feel that you have authority; the confidence and the gravitas to play that lead. Suddenly, you have to *lead* the company: that is why it's called 'the lead'.

I remember a couple of occasions in which actors in this situation initially struggled to 'step up'. On the first occasion it was the humility of the actor that made them reluctant to expand into the role. This actor was technically very competent and had confidence in their skills, but they didn't want to appear brash, overconfident or arrogant. My role in their development was to help them to feel that their technique and experience allowed them the stability, flexibility and confidence to take up more space on the stage, and that it served the play for them to do so. By focusing on technical work, they came to realise that authority didn't mean arrogance.

On the second occasion, the actor feared they would not make the friendships they were used to making when they were just part of the company. This played out in them being rather too jocular in rehearsals and seemingly not putting enough work into the preparation and rehearsing of their scenes. My impression was that they were apologising for their success. As such, my work with them was to bring focus into the interpretation of their role through our technical work on voice and the text of the play. This helped them to remember that the production and the other actors needed them to be playing at the top of their game for the production to be successful.

It was a difficult journey for both actors. Modern British theatre tends to distrust the so-called 'star system'. Veneration of the leading actor is strongly resisted, even if that actor is famous and has been cast to attract an audience. Any actor who behaves as if they are special will not be popular or respected. Instead, we embrace what is called the 'company feel'. Actors in British drama schools are trained in ensemble (collaborative) work. They learn that acting is essentially a team sport and for the production to be a real success, the whole company has to work together on equal terms, whatever the size of their role. However, in both these situations, the actors needed to find the authority within themselves to lead their productions, while still feeling part of the team. This is not something that always comes naturally.

Where do actors find this authority? That is what this section of the book will explore. As we will see, the first step to communicating with authority involves being in control of your situation. With both first-time lead actors, my work with them emphasised taking the focus off themselves and their insecurities, and placing their attention where it was needed: on the play and how they could best perform their leading role. It is an approach we can all learn from. In every situation, confidence – and authority – will come from feeling in control of your thoughts, your voice and your presence.

ACTIVE LISTENING, ACTIVE SPEAKING

Good listening is such an important part of effective communication; a skill that will help you to feel present and in control, as well as having a significant impact on how you breathe and speak. In fact, listening is linked in some way to everything I talk about in this book. Mark Gatiss told me about an early lesson he was taught by his 'childhood hero' Jon Pertwee – the renowned stage and TV actor perhaps best known as the third incarnation of Doctor Who – who he worked with early in his career. His key lesson for Mark was also the simplest: 'Don't force anything. Just listen.'

Good actors, like Jon Pertwee and Mark Gatiss, know they need to be present and aware of everything that is happening around them. This is true for any kind of performance: the best presenters will be attentive to what has been said earlier in the meeting and will adapt their language in response; the best speechmakers will be acutely aware of how the audience is responding to what they say, so they can adjust their delivery. An important part of being able to do so is *active* listening. This approach emphasises focusing on and finding clarity in what the person you are listening to is saying, so you are better able to take in information and move the conversation forward. (The opposite is passive listening, when the mind isn't focused on the person speaking. This usually means your mind is either full of other thoughts or you are focused on how you will be affected by what you hear.)

A good place to start listening actively is with your centred posture. This will make you alert and will give the right message to the person speaking: that you are attending closely to what they are saying. If your weight is falling backwards, you will look less interested and you will find it harder to engage. If you are pushing your weight forward, it will seem as if you are keen to interrupt. Then, with your head centred, make eye contact. I once had a colleague who, in conversation with me, would look away as soon as I began to speak. It always felt insulting, as if what I had to say was boring or of no value (maybe it was, but they should have listened anyway!). Making eye contact, on the other hand, will not only let the speaker know you are listening – it will help you to focus on them.

From there, you will need to concentrate hard to avoid becoming distracted; your own thoughts and ideas will intrude but try to put them on hold in order to attend to the speaker. Above all, try not to second-guess the speaker's points. I have a friend who often tries to finish my sentences for me, which is a common urge when trying to show that you are engaged. But it doesn't work; my friend's guesses are never right. Better to refrain from jumping in, passing judgement or giving advice, unless it's asked for. Instead, ask questions. Remember that you should be listening to understand a point of view, to learn something or perhaps to enjoy what is being said.

Active listening also involves becoming more aware of physical cues. You'll know if you are listening well by your speaker's body language: are they relaxing? Are they maintaining eye contact with you? By noticing their non-verbal language, you might also understand things they aren't saying. Do they seem to want to leave the room? Do they find eye contact difficult? If they fold their arms on their chest, are they blocking an idea or showing disinterest? Are they tapping their fingers or foot, showing impatience? Are there things they want to say but can't? Could you ask the right question to help them to speak?

One exercise I do with actors is designed to cultivate all these skills simultaneously. When working on a piece of dialogue, I ask each actor to repeat the last word or two, or last phrase of the other character's speech, before they speak their lines in reply. The idea is to ensure that you have properly heard what has just been said before jumping in with a response. This works in conversation too: you could try to repeat in your mind those last words spoken by the previous speaker before you reply. It will ensure that you let them finish their point and that you are replying first to what they have said before making any contribution of your own.

Being active does not just extend to listening, however. Active speaking has become a buzzword in British theatre; we talk about speaking and using language *actively*. By this we mean that everything an actor says should 'act on' or affect the character or characters they are talking to; that is, they should be trying to persuade them to do something: to agree with them, to change their mind, to rile them or appease them, for example. This idea was defined and developed from the work of Stanislavski, by director Max Stafford-Clark with his companies Joint Stock and Out of Joint. In his book *Letters to George*, he explains how it is used in the company's rehearsal process. The technique is to choose a transitive verb – a verb that does something *to* another character or characters – to describe what you will be trying to do with the section of text you are about to speak. That could be 'I recruit you' or 'I surprise you', 'I ennoble you' or 'I seduce you' for example. These are referred to as your 'actions'.

In Out of Joint rehearsals, the actors would speak their chosen verb before speaking the piece of text it refers to. By the time they come to perform the play, they will have dropped the speaking of the verb but retained its meaning. The method keeps the focus on what their character wants to achieve, moment by moment and throughout the play. It also means that the play is spoken very clearly. For example, Danny Sapani worked with the company in 2004, playing Macbeth in a version of the play influenced by contemporary events in Central Africa. The transitive verbs 'focus the storytelling', Danny explains. 'Max understood that you need to bring the whole audience in.' He recounted how they did the actioning exercise as a group, so that they all knew everyone's intention and could all contribute to the choices being made.

In my experience, this 'transitive verb' technique is useful for anyone making a speech or presentation. The National Theatre's current Director, Rufus Norris, trained as an actor at RADA. When he was preparing to make a speech at the end of a big fundraising gala, he asked me to hear him practise and advise him. He was familiar with 'actioning' and speaking actively from his training, and so was able to use the technique to clarify the aims of each section of the speech and energise them with clear 'actions'. I'm not suggesting that you need to think of transitive verbs every time you speak (although you could try that). But it can be helpful to ensure that with every sentence you are clear about your aims and intentions – and in turn fully in control of your communication.

Exercise 1: Active speaking

To help you focus on how you wish to affect your listeners moment by moment, you could try this exercise which many actors use in rehearsals. Looking at your written text, think about what you are trying to do with each thought or section. Then write above the section, or in front of it, the relevant verb. It could be 'tempt' or 'entice', 'inform' or 'intrigue', 'challenge' or 'reassure', for example – use whatever feels right.

To illustrate this, here is how we might 'action' a section from the suffragette Emmeline Pankhurst's 'Freedom or Death' speech, delivered at Hartford, Connecticut on 13 November 1913:

Excite: *I am here as a soldier who has temporarily left the field of battle in order to explain – it seems strange it should have to be explained – what civil war is like when civil war is waged by women.*

Intrigue: *I am not only here as a soldier temporarily absent from the field at battle; I am here – and that, I think, is the strangest part of my coming.*

Warn: *I am here as a person who, according to the law courts of my country, it has been decided, is of no value to the community at all: and I am adjudged because of my life to be a dangerous person, under sentence of penal servitude in a convict prison.*

Conspire: *So you see there is some special interest in hearing so unusual a person address you.*

Amuse: *I dare say, in the minds of many of you – you will perhaps forgive me this personal touch – that I do not look either very like a soldier or very like a convict, and yet I am both.*

When you are practising the speech, you might actually speak the verbs before you speak the words. Then practise again without speaking the verbs, but with the memory of the action.

VOCAL ENERGY

In 2010, Sir Nicholas Hytner, then the Director of the National Theatre, directed *Hamlet* with Rory Kinnear in the title role. On the first day of rehearsals, Nick told the company that, although he hadn't yet mentioned it to me, he wanted a lot of the play to be spoken quite quietly. The production was going to be played in the Olivier Theatre. When I spoke to him about this direction, I learned that he wanted the production to sound modern and not be over-spoken or over-presented. I was delighted to hear that, as I too wanted the actors to sound easy and contemporary. Nick has a good ear for the actors' voices and the way they use the text of a play; he is very alert to whether or not they can be heard and understood well.

My challenge was to make sure that the actors were speaking the text naturally, easily and sometimes quite quietly and yet could still be heard in the Olivier. That meant focusing first on ensuring they were able to sustain their vocal energy through any given line or speech. Have you ever been to a play and suddenly realised you've missed a bit, even when you thought you were listening closely? Or struggled to hear everything actors were saying on stage or on film or TV? Have you sometimes felt the actors were swallowing parts of their lines? There could be many reasons for this, some of which the actors have no control over: a musical underscore that is just too loud, or a lighting scheme that is too dark for you to be able to see the actors' faces, for example. However, the fault might also be with the actor and how they maintain the energy of their voice through the text. They will not be able to carry authority in their performance if they are unable to commit to and sustain the energy of their voices, even when they are required to speak quite quietly.

In this section, then, I am going to show you how I teach actors to maintain vocal energy when they also need to be absorbed into the fictional reality of their part and the play – precisely the kind of work that I did with those actors in *Hamlet* to powerful effect. The clarity and naturalness of their speech was a crucial factor in the critical success of this modern dress production, which was praised for its 'detailed political, social and psychological context'. And the same tools will help bring clarity and naturalness to any speech that you might need to deliver.

My first step was to help the actors to be very clear about their characters' thinking. When we are talking about spoken delivery, it is not only voice that counts but also your commitment to the ideas you are presenting. Therefore, with actors, I often begin our work by looking at how their character might structure their thoughts. In acting, we focus on 'thoughts' a great deal, to help actors to be specific with what they are saying. Referring to thoughts is a way of clearly identifying ideas and how we communicate them, and to be aware that each point we make may contain several ideas or thoughts. Considering what you want to say as a series of thoughts will be a useful way for you to make sure each of the points you are making are heard clearly and fully.

So the next few exercises work with thoughts, to show you how vocal and intellectual energy can work together. The first step is to find the thoughts within what you are saying: the simplest way to illustrate that is by using a text. Consider the opening speech of Shakespeare's *Richard III*, spoken by Richard. At the beginning of the speech, Richard is referring to what he thinks is the end of the Wars of the Roses, during which the two powerful families of York and Lancaster have been fighting over the English crown. The House of York won the recent Battle of Tewkesbury and Edward IV, Richard's brother, has now replaced Henry VI as king.

We are going to divide this piece of writing into individual 'thoughts'. It's up to the reader where each thought begins and ends. They may be contained within a single sentence, or they may go over several sentences. For example:

Thought one:

Now is the winter of our discontent
Made glorious summer by this sun of York,

Thought two:

And all the clouds that lour'd upon our house
In the deep bosom of the ocean buried.

Thought three:

> *Now are our brows bound with victorious wreaths,*
> *Our bruised arms hung up for monuments,*

Thought four:

> *Our stern alarums changed to merry meetings,*
> *Our dreadful marches to delightful measures.*

Thought five:

> *Grim-visaged war hath smooth'd his wrinkled front,*
> *And now, instead of mounting barbed steeds*
> *To fright the souls of fearful adversaries,*
> *He capers nimbly in a lady's chamber*
> *To the lascivious pleasing of a lute.*

Or, you could divide it like this:

Thought one:

> *Now is the winter of our discontent*
> *Made glorious summer by this sun of York,*
> *And all the clouds that lour'd upon our house*
> *In the deep bosom of the ocean buried.*

Thought two:

> *Now are our brows bound with victorious wreaths,*
> *Our bruised arms hung up for monuments,*
> *Our stern alarums changed to merry meetings,*
> *Our dreadful marches to delightful measures.*

Thought three:

> *Grim-visaged war hath smooth'd his wrinkled front,*
> *And now, instead of mounting barbed steeds*
> *To fright the souls of fearful adversaries,*
> *He capers nimbly in a lady's chamber*
> *To the lascivious pleasing of a lute.*

The difference between these two approaches might seem minimal but the way we divide our thoughts has a significant effect on how it is performed – as the following exercise shows.

Exercise 2: Finding a thought structure

Speak the speech aloud holding your text in one hand. When you come to the end of a thought, change hands before you speak the next one. You can choose which thought structure to use: personally, I love a long thought, but you could choose either, or try both. When you have tried the speech changing hands, then repeat it without changing hands.

How does each version of the speech feel? Are you unfolding your ideas through these thoughts, laying them out for your listener to take in and absorb? Can you retain the journey of the thoughts but without chopping them up or labouring them?

After you have tried the exercise with this speech, give it a go with a piece of your own. Again, it could be something you have to present, or another piece of text that has some sort of point to make: a piece from a newspaper, a book or a play perhaps. When you are clear about where thoughts begin and end, you could mark them in the script, if you have one.

Once you have identified how thoughts work, it is also important that you 'land' the thought. In theatre, we often talk about 'landing' an idea, a thought, a word or a sentence. By this, we mean that we deliver our point into the ears and minds of the listeners without rushing on to a new point. Even if you are speaking quickly, each thought *must* land, with the last word or two of your thought being clearly spoken and clearly heard. It is very common for speakers, including actors, to simply drop their vocal energy on the last word or two of a thought or a sentence, even when they have enough breath. The habit comes about from a lack of control, when someone is not speaking with clear intentions, and so moves on from point to point too quickly.

In order for your thoughts to be delivered successfully, they have to be heard and understood from beginning to end. When they work with Shakespeare, actors are taught to recognise the importance of the last word written at the end of a line of poetry or at the end of a sentence. But it's not just in Shakespeare that the last word of a thought might be the most important one, and when you are thinking and speaking quickly it is very easy, in your enthusiasm, to rush over it and on to the next sentence or the next thought.

The following exercises will help you to land your thoughts. The first is very familiar to actors; from drama school onwards, they find they have to work hard to keep their vocal energy and the energy of their articulation going to the very end of a thought or sentence. When you first try this, it might feel unnatural. But be assured that you won't sound unnatural as long as you make sure the last words of your thoughts land well, although you will have to practise it to become comfortable and confident.

Exercise 3: Supporting the end of your thought

Try this exercise with the piece of text you have divided into thoughts.

Speak it through aloud, and whenever you get to the end of a thought, tap your leg or the table as you speak the last word of the thought. The point of the exercise is to tap as you speak the word, so be careful that you don't tap slightly before or after. Don't over stress the word by banging on your leg or the table, just try to make enough contact to keep the word alive.

Do you feel how it makes you connect to that word so that you give it appropriate energy and meaning?

Now read the piece through again without tapping. Can you retain the same connection and energy?

Breathing, as so often, is another important factor to consider in making sure your voice is energised and able to sustain your words to the end of your thoughts. You must be sure that you are not trying to speak for too long on one breath. There has been a tradition in classical theatre training, especially when working with Shakespeare, to train actors to speak long sentences on one breath. There is some sense in this; it is important to be able to vocally sustain a character's thoughts and maintain persuasive energy. However, it can backfire. I remember an experienced actor who was performing in a Jacobean play several years ago. He had obviously learned to speak in long breaths, and in his youth the technique may have served him well. But at the time, his breathing and vocal stamina were a little diminished and the result was that he did not have enough breath to get to the end of each passage; the words had to be squeezed out of his throat. Listening to him was not as easy as it could have been – it made the listener concerned about him rather than hearing the play. If you tend to speak for too long without taking a new breath, it might seem that you are afraid to take one. That might be true: sometimes, you might worry that you will be interrupted before you have made your point or fear you will lose your listeners' attention if you pause for breath. But in most cases, it is better to be concise. Speaking more words doesn't mean you are saying more.

Having focused on the problem of running out of energy as you speak and so fading away at the end of a thought, we should also look at two habits I regularly come across concerning the beginning of a sentence or thought. One is holding the breath before you begin to speak; the other is rushing your first few words.

It is always important to remember to take a breath before you begin speaking; if you don't, you may then not have enough to sustain your response. You may think that this is obvious, but breath holding is very common – it is completely normal to suspend your breath when you are listening to someone and thinking. This might happen when you are waiting for your turn to speak in a meeting perhaps or wanting to respond to a point in a conversation. The trouble is, if you don't then breathe before you speak you may not have enough breath to sustain your voice adequately. When you are holding your breath, your vocal folds are closed, holding back your breath, so when you eventually speak, the voice bursts out and you waste a lot of breath on your first few words. This brings about what I call 'boom and bust'; a big release of energy in the voice that then fades away, either losing vocal energy or dropping in pitch – or both.

The second issue is rushing the beginning of a thought. People often seem to want to get very quickly to the first stressed word or phrase of their thought. *Iwantyouto-knowthatintoday's* meeting *we* decided *thatthetimewas* right *tochange* direction. (Which meeting? You decided to do what to the direction?)

Tobeornottobethatisthe question. (What is the question?)

I often hear this when actors are playing Shakespeare. There seems to be an idea in some productions that, to make the plays modern and relevant, the words need to be spoken very quickly and very conversationally. There may be concern that the actors will be too reverential or poetic with the language and that the audience will switch off. The opposite is in fact true. When listeners can't keep up with the speed of speech, they get bored and lose any interest they had. This can happen to anyone who has forgotten to take a breath when they have something to say. It might happen to you when you are nervous to speak, or you fear that your point isn't important enough, or that you just don't want to take up too much time. As I tell actors, you need to hold your nerve not your breath. It doesn't take much time to take a breath and it also indicates that you are going to speak, and so draws attention towards you in a helpful way.

Now that you have become more aware of the importance of starting and finishing your thoughts clearly, we can move on to sustaining your vocal energy throughout the entire thought. This next exercise will help you to make your points with appropriate energy and purpose, and to ensure that you are always moving forward in your arguments. It will also show you that variety of rhythm and pace come when you work with the structure of your thoughts.

Exercise 4: Sustaining your voice through the structure of your thoughts

Try this exercise using a piece you are going to present. You should start by identifying each point you are making and dividing these points into thoughts.

Now, place two chairs as far apart as you can get them. Stand beside one of the chairs, then begin to read your first thought and at the same time, walk to the other chair.

Your aim is to take your first step on the first word of your thought, and to get to the other chair as you get to the last word of your thought. Depending on the size of the room you are practising in, you may have to walk slower or faster, and sometimes you may have to take a circuitous or longer route – but you must keep going, with the chair you are walking to always in your mental view as your destination.

When you reach the chair, turn and walk back to the first chair as you speak the next thought, and so on.

Even if you have to slow down for a longer thought, try not to lose your energy, your forward momentum. You need to keep a sense of intention going, so that you are always on the way to your destination.

When you have finished the exercise, read the piece again and see if you have found a structure that gives clarity and drive to your thoughts.

Being in control of your vocal energy and using it to deliver your thoughts, ideas, point of view or story, clearly and effectively, is an important element in communicating with authority. But you must practise these exercises to get the feel of the work in your body and voice, and you must practise speaking them aloud; thinking them, or speaking them quietly, will not help you. Remember that you are aiming to speak clearly with energy in your voice, even if it is at a conversational volume.

PACING AND PAUSING

Many years ago, in an early stage of my voice coaching career, I was asked by a tourist company to speak about

my job to a group of American visitors who were on a theatre holiday and who were seeing shows at the National
Theatre. I remember that as I was telling them about
what I thought were interesting elements of my work,
I gradually realised that several of them were dozing off.
I could see that I would have to change something to get
their interest: I was being paid, after all. I quickly tried a
different approach. I finished my point, paused, as if for
thought, and then launched back in as if I had just remembered something that would really interest them. I then
delivered my next point as if it were an anecdote.

I realised that in using this approach, I was talking *to*
them, not *at* them. With that pause came a new breath, a
change of energy and a change of tone, and they all woke
up. So as I carried on, I tried to make everything I related
sound as if I was sharing information especially for them,
because they knew about theatre – as well as continu-
ing to allow myself time to pause for my thoughts and
theirs for the rest of the speech. Sometimes I made them
laugh, at other times I was able to change the tone and
pace to tell them something more serious or give them
some facts. I came out of my own head space and into
theirs, and by doing so I gained their trust as well as their
interest.

The creative use of pacing and pausing is another way
you can stay in control, and so ensure that you are heard.
Earlier in this chapter, when I was discussing modern

versions of Shakespeare, I mentioned that speaking too fast can kill your audience's interest. This is not only because they need to hear and understand everything you say but also because they need time to absorb it. If you rush from point to point in your argument or story, your listeners will not have time to think about what you are saying, and you won't have time to deliver it well. When I spoke to Indira Varma about pace, she very pragmatically commented: 'You don't want the audience to overtake you, but keep up with you, because if they've missed what you've said, there's no point in carrying on.'

However, this is not to say that you can't think quickly or be enthusiastic in your delivery. Deborah Findlay told me how she admires actors who are 'witty and clever and can turn on a sixpence'. This is particularly true in comedy, where writers or performers often want to keep their listeners on their toes – creating humour from surprise, unexpected juxtapositions or analogies. You may not want to make jokes, but understanding how speed of thought can create excitement and engagement is a very useful tool in the communication workbox. It can be thrilling to hear someone so in control of their thoughts and their material that they are, at appropriate times, able to speak with great dexterity.

But these moments need to be well judged and handled with skill, and you will have to be on top of your articulation. Using speed cannot just be about varying your pace; you must be sure you are trying to engage your listeners and that the change of pace reflects the tone and energy of what you are delivering at that moment. Can you keep the sense of talking to your listeners when you increase your speed? Can you be sure to land every thought?

If you are working on a speech or presentation and feel that one portion needs to move with particular speed and energy, you should still consider finding places to pause. You may be moving with speed from point to point, making sure you have landed each one, but there must come a moment when you pause; when you can afford to give a little space for the audience to absorb what they have heard, and hopefully, to admire your ideas and agree with them. Be sure to take a pause before you introduce a new topic, giving your listeners a bit of time to consider the conclusion of your previous topic. It is also helpful to pause after you have emphasised something; again, it allows your audience time to take the information in. When you do pause, you will also find that the bit of space you have created will allow you to take a fresh breath to begin your next point. Fresh breath will always bring fresh energy to what you are saying, and therefore how you say it and how it is heard. The following exercise will help you to find the right pace, changes of pace and pauses in your speech, presentation or story.

Exercise 5: Imaginary conversations

When I'm working with actors on a speech, I sometimes turn it into a conversation by sitting or standing in front of them as they deliver the speech to me.

As they go through the speech, at the end of thoughts, I will voice what the audience might be thinking. This might be something like: 'Oh! That's interesting, tell me more', or 'Really! Is that true?', or 'That's odd/funny/shocking', or just 'Yes', 'No!', 'Aha', 'I hear you', or even 'I don't get it, say it again'. I then ask the actor to repeat the speech without me speaking, but with the memory of my thoughts.

Ask a trusted friend or your partner to do the same for your speech, responding to each new thought you land. Alternatively, you can do the exercise alone, imagining in your head what your listeners might be thinking and leaving a bit of space for those thoughts.

The point here is that once you have considered your breathing, the best way to find variety of pace and tone is to be sure that you are talking *to* your audience – not just delivering your speech.

CONTROLLING YOUR COMMUNICATION

I recently worked with someone who works as a consultant. The basis of her work was talking to her clients, and she regularly made presentations to large groups of people in person as well as on radio and TV. She had been working in this way for many years very successfully, and in the past, had been confident in and praised for her way of speaking and presenting. She had come to see me, however, because she had lost confidence in this ability, finding herself getting very anxious in the lead-up to a presentation. She appeared tense and spoke very fast and at great length, not allowing me to easily enter into a conversation about the problem.

I suggested that up until recently, she had winged her way through her public speaking work by depending on her enthusiasm for her ideas. As she had grown older, she had become more aware of herself in the work, and the adrenaline that had previously supported her speaking now manifested as anxiety. My plan to help her was to teach her the lessons I am offering you. We began with how her voice and body worked and I gave her exercises to help her gain control over her breath and voice. Then I moved into the areas that would bring back her sense of her own authority: listening, remembering what her intentions were, sustaining vocal energy, landing her thoughts, and the imaginary conversation exercise.

The effects were rapid. In the course of these exercises, my client began to feel more in control of how she communicated. She practised at home and soon I could see the changes in her body – her shoulders had dropped and her head was more poised. I could tell that her breathing was more relaxed as we could have easy conversations instead of her rapid monologues. She told me that she did a little preparation before each speaking event and made sure her body was free enough to breathe and speak easily, and she said the improvements had been noticed by her working partners. She said she found it enormously helpful to have practical things to do to support her work.

This is the effect of the methods introduced in this chapter. Each one has been designed to put you in control of what you are saying and how you say it. Being confident that you can deliver your speech or other material effectively will lower your anxiety levels, and this in turn will allow you to speak with authority.

It is a powerful skill to possess. The authority that charismatic people have is not oppressive. Theirs is a power that comes from being in control of their speech and their ideas and from knowing how to engage with people. Whether or not you are an actor, understanding good communication skills and taking control of them will mean that you can build a sense of authority that will be apparent to both you and the people you engage with, one that leaves everyone feeling relaxed, receptive and confident.

CHAPTER 4

OWNING THE ROOM

A little forward of the centre of the stage in the Olivier Theatre, there is an acoustic 'hotspot'. Speaking from that spot, your voice is amplified by the structure of your surroundings; you hear it ring out.

This spot has become affectionately known as the 'Michael Bryant spot'. Michael was a superb actor who had a long career in theatre and performed many, many times in the Olivier. He was equally at home and in control whether playing Badger in *The Wind in the Willows*, Iago in *Othello*, or an enigmatic Teddy in Harold Pinter's *The Homecoming*. Watching him and hearing him speak from that stage taught me so much about how the acoustic of the room should be managed. He would place himself in the hotspot whenever he had a speech or soliloquy, and from there, with minimal movement and apparent effortlessness, he could command the room. He had an extraordinary presence on stage, drawing the audience to him and into the story. His apparent ease was deceptive; he was technically brilliant – centred, with great breath control and immaculate clarity of thought and word.

The Olivier Theatre is modelled on the ancient theatre at Epidaurus in Greece. The auditorium is a slight semi-circle, and the circular stage is what is called a 'semi-thrust' stage, meaning it pushes out into the front of the auditorium and the seating wraps around it a little at the sides. It has two levels, stalls and circle, and holds over 1,000 seats. When you are on the stage, because of its semicircular shape, the audience seems quite close to you. But from the auditorium, especially the circle, the stage seems very far away. This is deceptive for the actors, so when I took them into the theatre to understand how they would play in it, I would always make sure they went into the auditorium to experience how the audience would see them.

The question any actor playing on the Olivier stage faces is simple: how to ensure that the audience feels engaged with the play, despite its size? As Tamsin Greig recalls of her first time working there: 'I remember going on to that stage and being utterly overwhelmed by the size of it; seeing over 1,000 seats and thinking: how would you ever connect with all of those people?' However, Debra Gillett told me that once you start playing in there, you realise that 'the stage is so well designed that the "house" feels quite intimate'. When a show is going well and the actors are all engaged with each other and communicating the story, 'the audience become another member of the cast . . . I can feel them getting an idea, realising a gag, feeling anger or joy, and the silence of a full auditorium at a moving moment can be heart stopping'.

To achieve this, the actors must find an effective way to relate to the space. As Tamsin put it, she now feels that the connections happen if you 'surrender yourself to the space . . . making yourself available to what might happen'. She described a theatre as 'a full-empty space' – a place that, even without an audience, is charged with 'a mass of potential energy' in the anticipation of an event. Before every performance, she goes on to the stage to do her warm-up – but also goes into the auditorium 'to change places with myself on stage and myself as an audience member'. It may only be for ten minutes, but by doing so she gives space and time to being present there. This is what Michael Bryant was able to do so well; his many years of experience in the Olivier Theatre had taught him how to make his presence felt and his words heard by everyone.

In this chapter we are going to consider how to ensure that you, like the actors, can become familiar with the physical elements and the dynamics of any space in which you are to 'perform'. It takes confidence to be truly present – to 'surrender to the space', as Tamsin put it. But there are methods that can help. First, we are going to look at how to relate to a space in a way that gives you a sense of natural authority. Next, we'll explore how to draw your audience to you, to help them engage with you and what you are saying. Finally, we will explore the very different challenges of speaking online or on film and video – a very different kind of 'stage', but a stage nonetheless.

Your aim in all these situations is to feel comfortable with your audience and make them feel comfortable with you. Whenever you are speaking – not just to an individual in conversation but also when you are addressing a group of people – it is worth keeping in mind that you are in an exchange. Although listeners might not be replying, the very act of listening is a type of exchange, and to find the right energy for that exchange to happen effectively, it is vital that you take command of the room in which you are to speak.

TAKING COMMAND OF THE ROOM

Many years ago, a director I knew decided that to become a better director, he needed to experience what actors did. So he took a leading role in a play that was to be put on in a West End theatre. It was a daunting step: he had some experience of performing, but not in a play. And so, to support this new adventure, he asked me to give him some voice lessons.

Watching him develop his new skills was fascinating. He proved to be a very able actor but in the first preview I don't think the audience ever saw his face. He was terrified of looking out towards them, instead looking to the side of the stage, the back or to the floor. He was hiding from the audience. But without seeing his face, it was very difficult to know who the character was – and therefore to engage with him.

To help him, we ran some of the scenes with the rest of the company. But instead of playing just on the stage, I asked them to spread out through the auditorium: in the stalls, the circle, the upper circle and the gallery. They had to talk to each other across the whole theatre. After they had been playing a scene like this for a while, they gradually came back on to the stage and continued the scene there. This exercise helped our actor/director feel more confident looking out – and, when appropriate, speaking out – towards the audience. It also helped all the actors to claim the theatre as their own space, to command the room and fill it with the right amount of vocal and physical energy.

For me, the experience was a powerful reminder of what it truly means to 'own the room'. To really engage your audience, you need to share yourself with them. I wasn't encouraging this first-time actor to play his part in an unnatural way or to directly address the audience – it wasn't that sort of play – but to stand up, look up and take command of the theatre. This approach is equally useful for anyone who wants to command a space. However, that doesn't mean you necessarily dominate a room or an event. There will be some situations where you will be sharing the space, as actors do. You might be in an interview, a conversation or on a panel, for example. But you will be more able to command the room if you are familiar with and open to it as a physical space; are aware of its dimensions and are comfortable with your place within it.

A good starting point is to spend some time in the room before you must perform there. Like Tamsin Greig, many actors like to go into the auditorium in advance of the play. They need to feel that their working space is not just the stage; they want to feel connected to the auditorium, to feel the size of it in order to be able to play at the right level for that particular theatre. As Deborah Findlay tells me, you need 'just to get a measure of the space every time you come in, because you're coming in from a different world, aren't you?' Justine Mitchell does something similar, walking around the auditorium so that she can 'see what the audience are going to be seeing'.

This insight applies well beyond the theatre. If you are to connect with people in a large group, as a speaker at a meeting or a conference for example, it can help to go into the room where you are going to speak and get to know it. It will help you to know how much or how little you should move around to engage the whole audience. Being in the audience area will let you understand how you will be seen and heard and allow you to feel in control of the space. You will be able to view the stage or speaking area from different parts of the auditorium and notice if there are seats where the audience might find it more difficult to focus on you; seats that you need to make sure you include in the conversation. As you do all this, try to see things from the audience's point of view. Even if you don't have the privacy to try out your voice, spending time in the area you will speak from, and crossing over into the audience area, will help you to feel that you and the audience are in the same room and are going to be concerned with the same issues, entertainment or story. This simple action can take you a long way towards owning the room and feeling that the space is yours.

At some point during a voice warm-up on stage, I usually ask the actors to 'breathe the space', another exercise that I inherited from my predecessor at the National Theatre, Patsy Rodenburg. Based on one of Stanislavski's exercises, this is a technique that you can do formally, in preparation for a keynote speech or presentation. But you can also do it discreetly, as you walk into the room, or while you are in the company of others and need to feel you have a place at the table.

Exercise 1: Breathe the space

From the stage, platform or wherever you are standing or sitting, look out into the auditorium, hall or room. Focus on the furthest reaches of the space and imagine you are taking your oxygen from those far reaches, and that with that oxygen, you are breathing in the energy of the room. When you breathe out, send your energy back out into it on your breath. I suggest you choose points on the back wall to breathe to, and then different seats.

As well as giving you a sense of communicating with the whole room, this exercise will help you to expand into it physically and vocally. It will help you feel in command of the room and that you have the authority to speak to everyone in it.

Having become acquainted with your performance space, try to focus on the more practical elements of your presentation or speech. If possible, you should take the time to make sure you are comfortable with your set-up. Do you want a lectern? If you have one, is it in the right place? Is it a comfortable height? Is there a microphone? Do you need a chance to test it with a sound technician, or just to look at it to see its shape? (If it is flat-topped, you have to speak directly into the top of it. If it is round, you have more flexibility with how you speak into it.) Where is it placed and is its height easily adjustable? If you are able to explore the auditorium or seating area of your 'performance' space, the questions you should ask yourself are:

- How close should I stay to my table, chair or lectern? How will I best be able to communicate with my audience?
- If furniture has already been put in place for you, does it look right? If the stage area is very big, grouping furniture close together will make you seem small. But you will also need to focus the attention of your audience so it shouldn't be spread too wide.
- Is it too far back or too far forward? Would it be better on one side so that you have space to walk around if you wish?

Commanding the room means you have to be on top of your subject and be in control of how you speak and converse. But taking control of your physical environment will also help you to feel a sense of authority within it and be more prepared to meet your listeners there.

SPEAKING TO YOUR AUDIENCE

The convention in most modern theatre is that the front edge of the stage should be considered a 'fourth wall' to the scene – a concept that has been attributed to the eighteenth-century French philosopher and playwright, Denis Diderot. The actors concentrate upon the world they are creating within the confines of the stage, using natural speech and natural movements that are focused on each other, ignoring the audience. Generally, if the actors are looking out into the audience from a room, they will decide where a window might be and that they are looking through that. Or, if they are supposed to be outside, they will look at a particular landscape.

This does not mean that the audience is being ignored, though. Actors and directors employ 'stage craft' to balance the need of the audience to see and hear everything, with their desire to tell the story as naturalistically as possible. Through stage craft, actors can make sure audiences see their faces enough to be able to hear them and witness their expressions and their thinking, while seeming to be entirely focused on the other actors in the scene. They become aware, often with the assistance of the voice coach, of the furthest reaches of the auditorium and try to include every member of the audience in the production. This is not easy. Adjoa Andoh described it as a 'sacred duty' to reach everyone in the room. 'People come with a real need and our job is to facilitate their hearts being touched, their minds being stimulated,' she said. 'You have to bring all your skills to create an authenticity that creates a heart-to-heart conversation, and that includes being heard in the gods' (the cheapest seats at the very top of the auditorium).

What techniques, then, can one use to address one's audience and ensure you are heard throughout a space? Some useful methods – which can be applied as readily in meetings and presentations as on stage – come from the work I do with actors on 'direct address'. This is a convention that is found in period and classical drama, including Shakespeare, when characters might share their thoughts with the audience, in a soliloquy or 'aside'. Actors often find these daunting, because it breaks the 'fourth wall' convention: suddenly, they are addressing the audience directly.

One useful method I teach for speaking a short comment or thought as an aside is to speak directly to one or two individuals rather than trying to include the whole audience. In this way, the audience member, and by association the audience as a whole, is drawn directly into the action. Indira Varma told me about using this method in a non-naturalistic play at the National: *Exit the King*, a work originally written by the Absurdist playwright, Eugène Ionesco, which had been adapted into a new version written and directed by Patrick Marber. Indira remembered that she was concerned about the asides. But, she said, 'the minute I actually engaged with audience members it was really helpful'. Above all, it made the experience less nerve-wracking: 'because it was so specific – sharing one thing with someone sitting there, it was less frightening. Then you can find another thought and send that to someone else.' You can draw upon this approach in any situation when you are addressing a large group; even when you are a solo speaker, it is never really a monologue but always a conversation – after all, there is no point in you being there without the audience.

For longer forms of direct address – a whole speech or presentation, rather than an aside – I teach the actors to mentally divide the audience into three sections, and make sure that they take in each section during their speech. You can make the division either left, centre, right; or front, middle, back. Then, as you go through the speech, turn your attention to each section, probably several times as you speak. Try to make this as smooth and natural as you can, varying the way you do it: side-side-centre mixed with centre-side-side, for example. You should be using this method throughout your speech but combining it with directly addressing individuals if you find an appropriate place to do so – when you want to make a witty, ironic or pointed remark, for example. I was once coaching a politician for his party conference address, and we agreed that some of his comments about the opposition party would be addressed to individuals or a small section of the audience, an approach that made these moments of the speech feel more prominent and humorous. The idea is that everyone should feel your attention is being given to them personally.

Above all, it is important not to slip into a 'them vs me' frame of mind, feeling that your audience are there to judge or criticise you. This is an instinct that even very experienced actors must continually battle. Indira told me that in her most fearful states she imagines that the audience is full of famous, talented actors and directors who are there to critique her performance. To help her manage what she knows is an irrational fear of her audience, she told me she will try to have a look at them either before she goes on stage, or, if she can, when she is on stage: 'It's OK to have a look,' she says.

This method, she tells me, can be transformative. By seeing your audience and knowing they are just a group of people like yourself, you have a chance to rid yourself of self-judgement and self-criticism – and in turn be more present.

WORKING ON VIDEO AND FILM

Since 2020, most of us have had to get used to a very different 'space' in which to perform: on video. When the

Covid pandemic hit and people around the world found themselves locked in their homes for months on end, suddenly lots of us had to get used to delivering presentations and even simply meeting friends via Zoom and Skype. These virtual 'stages' pose a very different set of challenges to anyone who wants to communicate with charisma. Fortunately, however, these challenges are ones that most actors are familiar with from working on film and TV.

Many of the actors I spoke to emphasised that this medium requires a wholly different set of skills to a stage. Debra Gillett puts it most simply. 'Film and TV need as much energy as theatre but vocally it has to be entirely naturalistic,' she says. 'Every nuance can be picked up by sound and camera; to just *be* is the discipline.' In the close intimacy of the screen, thoughts are easily read. Film and TV actors must understand the power and expressiveness of being in control of their body and using movement and gesture, carefully and precisely.

This approach is clearly relevant to anyone working on screen. The listener's focus is tightly on the screen and everything the person being filmed does can be registered and possibly scrutinised. We have all become aware of our backgrounds when meeting online, and know that we judge each other's homes and tastes, through our book collections, our photographs, art or interior decoration. But in this environment our performance can be scrutinised as intensely as our environment, especially because the camera is so tightly focused on us. It is therefore important to take control of how we use our bodies and our voices in the same way that we have learned to organise and present our backdrops.

What considerations should one bear in mind when working on video, then? Remember, as ever, that your goal is to build a relationship with your audience. Just because you aren't in the same room as your listeners, that doesn't mean that you don't have a physical relationship with them. The camera, the computer or phone screen is just a window through which you are communicating. Do you remember when we first began our work together, looking in a mirror to find out how you use your body? It is similarly wise to look in detail at how you are using your body online.

One useful method is to set up a meeting in your platform of choice, but don't invite anyone. You will then be alone on screen to consider how you are presenting yourself. First take a look at your physicality. Your body should be as poised and centred as it is when you are meeting person to person. Find a comfortable, upright chair and seating position. Try to avoid sitting on your bed or a soft sofa if you can, as you will have no support for your posture and will probably tend to slump. As always, you will be most in control if your body and head are centred, with your shoulders relaxed. You will also look better.

Remember how useful it is to have at least one foot on the floor to enable you to feel grounded and to be able to breathe and speak from your whole body. There is a tendency, when you know that the screen focuses on your face, to lose your connection with the rest of your body and for all your energy to push up and forward through your face. If that happens, you will lose the authority that comes when you are centred and breathing from your abdomen.

Once you are feeling centred but not fixed or rigid, consider how you are placed within the frame of your screen. Simon Trinder, who has had considerable experience of TV and film, told me that his first thought for any scene he's in is, 'what is the size of the frame?' – that is, the limit of what is being included in the shot at a particular moment of filming. Is it a wide shot, including other actors or a large part of the set or scene, or is it a close-up, focusing on his face or body? He will ask the director of photography: 'How big is the picture around me?' When he knows this, he can choose his gestures and how he uses his body to refer to things he's talking about. As he said, there's no point gesturing to something that is out of shot and so unseen by the audience. Many people would benefit from asking this question before an online meeting. Check the frame around you when you are preparing and notice how much room you have given yourself to move and gesture.

At its core, this is about the placement of the computer or phone's camera and your eyeline. The camera in most devices is placed above the screen. This means that when you look at the person you are talking to on the screen, which you will naturally do, you appear to be looking down, and your eyes can be a little obscured. It can be worth investing in a separate camera that you can place in a position that is level with your eyeline but that also enables you to keep the person you are talking to in view, or a stand that enables you to place your device at your eyeline. If you are stuck with your in-built camera, however, you should try to look at the camera as much as you can. To make this seem as natural as possible, you should raise your screen to eye level. You can do this simply by placing your device on a pile of books. Now, when you angle the screen down towards your face you will see that your eyeline rises and your eyes appear more open.

There are other issues that arise in online meetings that are quite different from a film or TV set. Most notably, people tend to push their face and often their hands into the screen. Would you push your face close to someone in a real-time meeting? Would you make gestures with your hands right up into their faces? I don't think so. It would be aggressive or at least pushy. It will also draw you away from your centre, as you will be leading from your head, shoulders and arms. I know that this habit probably occurs because people are trying to communicate – to reach out through the screen. Unfortunately, it doesn't work well (try it in your one-person meeting and see). At the same time, the opposite – retreating from the screen – is also unhelpful. When someone is too far back, they can appear nervous or disengaged. In fact, there seems to be an optimum position in relation to the screen. See if you can find it. Try pushing forward. Can you see the effect it has? Now try retreating. Can you see the moment when you have gone just too far back? See if you can find that optimum position, where you appear engaged with the onlooker but not pushing too far forward.

Once you have found the best position, you can move on to the next big question facing anyone who needs to perform online: movement. The most common habit I see in online meetings is the tendency to generate all movement and all physical and vocal energy from the shoulders. Coming back to your centre, breathing down into your abdomen and speaking from there will keep this in check. Of course, being centred doesn't mean you can't be animated. When conversing online, we still want to be able to read each other's physical cues as well as hearing our words. But we need to learn how to be economical with our movement while being animated when we want to be. During the Covid pandemic, Adjoa Andoh spent some time teaching RADA students online. She mentioned being concerned about how best to communicate through this two-dimensional medium and how to 'tailor our gestures'. The solution, she says, was to get very focused on what you are doing in order to keep your physical energy contained and controlled. Focusing on the screen and the people you are talking to will help you to 'tailor your gestures', keeping them within the frame. So, take care that you aren't gesturing for the room you are in rather than the screen. This is particularly tempting if you are in an online meeting with others in the same room.

Finally, as well as reflecting on how you look on screen, you should consider how you are speaking. Before an important online meeting or event, you should be vocally as ready as you would be in any other situation. Here is a short preparation exercise to help you focus.

Exercise 2: Preparing for online meetings

Place your feet flat on the ground. Shrug your shoulders. Centre yourself by feeling your weight on your sitting bones. Breathe down into your abdomen.

Give your face muscles a workout by scrunching and stretching. Yawn or stifle a yawn to stretch your throat and release any tension from the back of your tongue. Hum down through your voice from high to low a couple of times to waken up the range of your voice for expressive speech.

Now, it's time to put all this together. Go back to your personal Zoom room (or Skype, Microsoft Teams, or whatever it might be) and see how you look. As you try to find the perfect position, explore and experiment with your relationship to the screen and try out different distances. How are you framed? How much of your body is it useful to see?

Think too about movement. Would you like to be able to use your hands? There are also practical issues to explore. Do you need to refer to a paper or notes? You may need to open other windows on your screen – experiment with how you can do this without losing your poise or your centring. Try practising some conversation and see how it looks and feels to make necessary moves or gestures. You may feel a bit silly doing it alone, but this sort of preparation is as important as the preparation you do for any live presentation or performance.

Once you are feeling in control of how you look and behave on screen, why not ask your partner or a trusted friend to join you in the meeting and get some feedback. Ask them to check your volume, and if you are delivering your thoughts clearly from beginning to end; not rushing or running out of vocal energy at the end of thoughts. Are you keeping enough variety and expressiveness without overemphasising or are you tending to be monotone or flat? Are you landing your thoughts effectively? As always, once you are confidently in control of your voice and body, you will get the best results if you focus on your listener more than yourself.

The most peculiar element of working on screen, I have often found, is how exhausting it can be. You'd think that sitting alone with a screen requires less energy. In fact, the opposite seems to be the case. Adjoa told me that she found working on video for long periods 'sucks the life out of you'. So, if possible, you should try to factor in reasonable breaks whenever you find yourself spending a considerable part of your day on video calls. If you can't, it will be very beneficial to have a good physical stretch between calls. Do you remember the exercise in Chapter 1, where you flopped over from the waist and then rolled up through your spine? This is an excellent way to refresh yourself; it gets blood to your face and brain and realigns your body. Actors often do it before performing, as well as in breaks in rehearsal.

SELF-DISCIPLINE AND OWNING THE ROOM

Not long ago, I was telephoned by a director in the middle of a preview performance of his play. The leading actor was struggling with his voice, and it seemed likely he would lose it. This actor had turned down the opportunity to work with me in rehearsals to prepare him for his very demanding, emotional role. He had even chosen not to attend pre-show vocal warm-ups, feeling very confident that he didn't need any support. It turned out he was wrong. No one could have managed to perform the role eight times a week in the way he wanted without having the technical knowledge that allows the release of feelings and thoughts through the voice safely and effectively.

He was not unique. From time to time, I come across actors who are either untrained or not properly trained. They fear that focusing on any sort of technique will undermine their freedom and spontaneity in performance. They haven't experienced how the disciplined practice of technical work can support and liberate their creativity. As a result, they don't know how to be 'in their bodies', or how to breathe freely, and they don't understand that physical relaxation will allow them more freedom. Not being familiar with how their body and voice work best, they are less able to relax and be authoritative. Inevitably, I usually find myself working with this type of actor when this supposed freedom has led them to lose their voice.

The final method for owning the room, then, is also the simplest: the importance of discipline. As Tamsin Greig puts it, 'from discipline comes freedom'. In fact, for her, this is the common thread in all communication. 'In any conversation, whether it's on screen, on a bus, with our neighbour,' she tells me, 'I think it's an act of discipline to be in a place where you still everything else and focus.'

She recounts a conversation she had with a man who was a cantor in a synagogue. 'Sometimes, after all your discipline and practice, every now and then, what you offer is met by something other and at these moments, it feels like I'm not singing,' he told her. 'I'm being sung.'

Ultimately, the most important way to build your authority is to take these exercises and practise them. As the actors I have interviewed show, continued success has come through hard work and self-discipline. They practise their technical work to keep their bodies, voices and thinking up to scratch. They prepare thoroughly for rehearsals and for performances and they take seriously the environment they are to perform in. This allows them to act with true freedom; they don't have to push their performances and they only lose their voices if they have a cold.

It is this disciplined practice, preparation and attention to detail that allows actors to succeed. It gives them confidence in their ability to achieve their goals and the authority to carry them through. You too can experience the freedom that comes from discipline. And, like Tamsin's cantor, you might find yourself experiencing a very natural, embodied authority – and the song will sing you.

PART III
ELOQUENCE

CHAPTER 5

THE USE AND POWER OF RHETORIC

Friends, Romans, countrymen, lend me your ears

This is one of Shakespeare's most famous lines. It is the beginning of a funeral speech; an oration by Mark Antony in *Julius Caesar*. It is delivered shortly after the death of Julius Caesar, who has been murdered in the Senate. A group of senators had acted to stop Caesar increasing his power, which they believed would lead to the collapse of the Roman Republic and the establishment of a dictatorship. The group did not include Mark Antony, who was particularly close to Caesar. Antony wants revenge for the murder of his friend, but he doesn't want to show his hand (we later see that he has plans to gain more power himself). He therefore uses this speech to subtly move the crowd to revolt against the senators who were involved in the conspiracy.

The speech is well known and very clever. However, fewer people know that it follows a speech by Brutus, who was one of the murderers. This is the beginning of Brutus' speech:

Romans, countrymen and lovers, hear me for my cause, and be silent, that you might hear.

As Brutus has chosen to speak first, he has opened the way for Mark Antony to respond with a rhetorical trick; he has taken Brutus' words and changed them to his own advantage.

In *Julius Caesar* we see Shakespeare having a rhetorical field day. All his plays are full of rhetoric; characters use it, or try to use it, and they talk about it. In *Julius Caesar*, rhetorical skills are an integral part of the Roman world in which the play is set, and they are key to the central events of the play. Although we don't know for certain, we assume that Shakespeare attended the King Edward VI grammar school in his hometown of Stratford-upon-Avon. Rhetoric and classical languages were taught there, as they were a standard part of all schools' curriculum at that time; sixteenth-century England had a great interest in the classical world. In ancient Rome, the ability to be eloquent and persuasive was of huge importance to anyone who wanted to become part of the ruling elite. In *Julius Caesar* we see power struggles played out at the highest level, where clever, persuasive speech alongside social and political astuteness are matters of life and death.

Half a millennium after Shakespeare's time – and two millennia after Mark Antony's – the rhetorical methods he utilises remain compelling. Returning to the opening lines of these two key speeches, we can already see that they are going to differ greatly in tone. Brutus seems to command the people to be quiet and listen to him. Antony begins his speech with 'Friends' and he asks them to 'lend' him their ears. From the very beginning, he puts himself on a level with his audience, and he continues to do so throughout the speech. His tone is conversational, despite the fact that he speaks in verse. Brutus speaks in prose, yet his rhetoric is so formal as to appear almost formulaic. He isn't able to speak *to* the people; he seems to be speaking *at* them.

Brutus and Mark Antony were both close to Caesar, but they are very different characters. Brutus was descended from Consuls, the highest elected officials in the Roman Republic. He is constantly addressed as 'noble Brutus' and throughout the play he is shown to be confident in that nobility; we learn that he is admired by leaders and commoners alike. This perhaps lends him a certain arrogance. He is sure that if he speaks first and shows 'the *reason* of our Caesar's death', the people will be persuaded that the assassination was justified. He doesn't tailor his rhetoric to his audience; his speech seems formal and rather blunt.

At first, it looks like it has worked – and he seems to have won the crowd over.

However, Brutus' biggest mistake is allowing Mark Antony to speak at the funeral at all. Although also of noble rank, Antony is a soldier and is perhaps more used to speaking to men of lower rank. He is able to shift the support of the crowd in a different direction; to make the people again believe that a crime has been committed by Brutus and the other senators. He uses a tone that appears more conversational, yet his language isn't colloquial, and he is certainly eloquent. Most important of all is that he works on their emotions very effectively.

Both men are using rhetoric as developed in Ancient Greece and passed down through the centuries in Aristotle's treatise *On Rhetoric*. With the birth and development of democracy in Greece in the fifth century BC, the political and legal systems were open to any man who had the time, money and education to aspire to them. To cater to these new opportunities, specialists in public speaking emerged, some of whom taught and wrote on the subject. Many approached it philosophically, notably Plato, but it was Aristotle who formalised persuasive speaking, presenting it as a pragmatic tool, although he also considered it an art. It is his work that was studied by Shakespeare in school, and it influences writers and speakers to this very day.

However, today, rhetoric is often considered a dirty word, indicating cynical word play used by self-interested politicians to cover up or manipulate the truth. Of course, it can be used in that way. But rhetoric is about so much more. It is the 'art of persuasion'. As such, it can be used in any situation – to put across a point of view, to present an argument, to tell a story or even a joke, and sometimes to save a life. It is still relevant, and a little knowledge of its rules can help you to find the style, vocabulary and tone that will serve your own arguments and points of view.

I believe that every time an actor opens their mouth on stage, they are trying to persuade somebody of something. This is how plays work – people talking their way forward to some sort of change or catharsis. In other words, they are continually using rhetoric. This is also often the case in real life. We all use language strategically, not just in politics or business but in any situation where we need to speak clearly and persuasively. That could mean a wedding speech or a proposal. Or it could mean something altogether more everyday: a colleague told me they had recently used their knowledge of rhetoric to successfully persuade their builder to reduce his bill because the work being done was not up to standard. In many cases, it is something we understand intuitively, with our instincts telling us how we might shift an argument in our favour. Aristotle and the ancient scholars and philosophers didn't *invent* persuasive language, they just drew upon their observations of how we are influenced by words and ideas, then codified and exploited them.

In this chapter, we will see how rhetoric forms the basis of our third pillar of charisma: eloquence. This term captures a wide array of qualities. Speaking in a way that is fluent and persuasive; that catches and keeps the attention of listeners; that shows understanding of subject matter; and, at its best, also understands its audience and adapts in order to reach them. It can involve being as coldly rational as Brutus or as powerfully emotive as Mark Antony. And, as we will see in the pages to come, it is something that can be learned.

PERSUASIVE STRATEGIES

Aristotle taught that there are three main strategies you can use to persuade somebody of something.

The first strategy is to show your listeners they can trust you. You can do this by exhibiting knowledge of your subject, but also by letting your listeners know, or reminding them, who you are. You are presenting your credentials and your integrity. Brutus and Antony both do this as they speak of their love for Caesar and their respect for Rome.

The second is to make sure that you back up your argument or point with evidence, or present facts about outcomes. This is the intellectual, pragmatic way of making a point. It is largely what Brutus was using to present his argument. It appeals to rational thought, something that was very important among the intelligentsia of the Roman Republic.

The third strategy is to make your listeners feel something, to move their emotions in some way. With this strategy you could try to make them feel good about something, or you could make them angry or indignant. You could try to make them empathise with your subject or you could make them laugh or cry. And this is what Mark Antony was doing throughout his speech to such remarkable effect.

In Greek, Aristotle's three strategies are called ethos, logos and pathos:

- **Ethos:** your credentials
- **Logos:** the evidence
- **Pathos:** the emotional connection

Shakespeare used all these strategies in the orations from *Julius Caesar*. At first, the people of Rome believed Brutus' argument; that he had taken part in the assassination of Julius Caesar for the good of Rome. He made it clear that, in the balance, he felt it was the right thing to do.

If there be any in this assembly, any dear friend of Caesar's, to him I say that Brutus' love to Caesar was no less than his. If then that friend demand why Brutus rose against Caesar, this is my answer: Not that I loved Caesar less, but that I loved Rome more. Had you rather Caesar were living, and die all slaves, than that Caesar were dead, to live all free men?

He makes his position plain by setting out the evidence as he sees it; notice how he uses comparisons to make his point: 'Not this, but this.' It is balanced and appears well thought out, charged with both ethos and logos.

Mark Antony, on the other hand, understands that ethos will not win here. His argument cannot be about himself but about Caesar and, most of all, about Brutus. He wants the people of Rome to conclude that a crime has been committed. In line with the accepted form of the funeral oration, he tells stories of honourable events in Caesar's life and most famously, he interlaces his stories with a repeated phrase about Brutus: 'Brutus is an honourable man.'

In his speech, Brutus has several times referred to his own 'honour' and Antony picks that up and makes *honourable* the key word in his speech. This is a very effective rhetorical device – to take a word used by your opponent in a debate and turn it to your own advantage. Later he places the word *honourable* into phrases that work like a chorus or refrain, referring to Brutus and the other senators who killed Caesar, and as with the chorus of a ballad, the meaning changes according to what precedes it. He gradually sows seeds of doubt in the minds of the crowd by picking apart Brutus' reasons for the murder – Caesar's dangerous ambition. In so doing, we begin to hear irony creep into the mention of 'honour'.

> *When that the poor have cried, Caesar hath wept;*
> *Ambition should be made of sterner stuff:*
> *Yet Brutus says he was ambitious,*
> *And Brutus is an honourable man.*

Or later:

> *If I were disposed to stir*
> *Your hearts and minds to mutinous rage,*
> *I should do Brutus wrong, and Cassius wrong,*
> *Who, you all know, are honourable men*

And finally, more pointedly:

> *I fear I wrong the honourable men*
> *Whose daggers have stabbed Caesar; I do fear it.*

By skilfully repeating the word and this phrase and changing the context, he is slowly and subtly playing his hand, and by doing so gradually turning the crowd.

There is logos in Antony's argument as he brings out evidence of Caesar's greatness. There is plenty of ethos too, in that he presents himself as a humble man who was

Caesar's friend. But it is by wringing out the pathos of his death that Mark Antony wins round his audience. He shows the people the blood-stained garment that Caesar was wearing when he was killed. He points out bloody cuts in the material where the knives went in and he imaginatively re-enacts the deed, naming senators who stabbed Caesar. He tells a version of the story of the murder to move his listeners to pity. His final strike is also pathos, when he produces and reads from Caesar's will – and reveals that Caesar has left his orchards to the citizens of Rome. The scene ends with the crowd running off, first to Caesar's cremation, and then to burn down the houses of the conspirators.

One need not be trying to stir up the crowds of ancient Rome to draw upon these methods; they are just as useful in our day-to-day lives. If you're trying to persuade your partner to go with you on that luxury holiday, or perhaps win a political argument with friends over a few drinks in a bar, for example. And they can be particularly powerful in more formal situations when used to focus a presentation, a sales pitch, a lecture, a speech or even a sermon. I'll show you some examples.

Many people like to begin with ethos as it sets out why they have the authority to make their case. But it's important to use ethos carefully and strategically, lest the argument or the point someone is making becomes all about them. I recently worked with an industry leader who was preparing to speak to his whole company. He was so keen to present himself as 'just one of the guys, who by hard work had made good', that the whole speech appeared self-reverential; it was all ethos. His intention was very credible, but he was trying to sustain it for too long. By helping him shift his focus away from himself and on to his audience, his delivery changed – so that speaking of his accomplishments served as an inspiration to the individuals who worked in his organisation, rather than as a celebration of himself.

Most good arguments will contain some logos, but sometimes the use of factual evidence might seem to dominate an assignment. A couple of years ago, I was asked to work with a member of the National Theatre finance team who had to present the figures and statistics of a financial initiative at a national conference. She had never presented before and was understandably nervous. More than her anxiety about being able to present her work fluently, she was anxious about her ability to make the figures and their implications clear in this spoken context. She was afraid she would bore her listeners. She was right to worry: it was a challenging task, and when she first read the script to me, I couldn't follow it. She spoke with a tone and pace that suggested that she knew her piece was dull, and that she was unimportant, so she should get through it as quickly as possible. She seemed to assume that no audience would find it interesting. She was caught in a tangle of self-consciousness and lack of belief in the interest of her material (although she knew its value).

My solution was to reframe her piece in terms of a persuasive argument; to focus on the specific purpose of the facts – the outcome. In this way, the figures weren't a difficult list to get through but the logos that supported this particular financial strategy. We sandwiched the logos of the figures between ethos and pathos. We began with ethos, the values of the National Theatre, and concluded with a touch of pathos, to enthuse her listeners with the success of the project and its potential for their organisations. We rewrote very little of it; the success of the presentation was in her understanding of how to shape and deliver the material she already had in an engaging and interesting way.

There is a great deal of rhetoric heard today that is sadly lacking in logos, or if used it is based on lies and fabrications. Unfortunately, it is often persuasive. I'm not suggesting you lie, but simply pointing out that logos is a strategy that can be manipulated to support any argument. Most of us will be selective with our choice of evidence; part of the fun of arguing with friends is to see how far your point of view can withstand opposition. In whatever situation you are presenting a line of reasoning, you need to know your facts. If they are vague, they won't carry the power of logos.

But perhaps the most effective method is pathos. It is a very powerful rhetorical strategy, which is why so many speakers have centred their political speeches on pathos, from Shakespeare, Patrick Henry, Churchill and Hitler to Martin Luther King, Bob Geldof and Donald Trump, with the effect of rousing their listeners to a united and passionate response. But it is not only in literature and politics that this strategy is effective. In the workplace, it is with pathos that you will stimulate the imaginations of your listeners. Once they are sure that you are credible, and they have seen or heard evidence of the validity of your idea, plan or product, it is their imaginations that will persuade them to buy or buy into it. They need in some way to be excited, to feel good about outcomes or products. To *feel* that things will be better because of what they hear from you. Pathos will also make you appear more charismatic in your day-to-day life, particularly if in your general conversations and debates you can persuade people that what you propose or support will make their lives or experiences better. Because pathos focuses on the feelings of your listeners it suggests an empathy with them, which is always appealing.

PUTTING ETHOS, LOGOS AND PATHOS TOGETHER

Of course, the best persuasive strategies will draw on elements of all three methods. I worked on a production of

Othello a few years ago and the actor playing the title role asked for help to find clarity in some of his big speeches. The play is set in Venice, which at the time was a city-state and a major centre of finance and trade. Othello, a black man from North Africa, is a general in the Venetian army who has had great success in various wars. During a period of peace, he has become friends with one of the senators of Venice, who has encouraged him to speak about his life, travels and adventures. The senator's daughter, Desdemona, falls in love with Othello through hearing these stories and they marry in secret. In Act 1, Scene 3, Othello is speaking to her father Brabantio and other Venetian senators, in defence of his marriage – using a masterful combination of ethos, logos and pathos to make his points. But the individual playing Othello – a splendid, talented actor – was initially unable to unpick the structure of the speeches. As listeners, we got rather lost and couldn't hear the argument.

I was able to show him how masterfully Othello used the three rhetorical strategies, beginning with logos – the facts of the matter:

Most potent, grave and reverend signiors,
My very noble and approved good masters,
That I have ta'en away this old man's daughter,
It is most true; true I have married her;

152

The very head and front of my offending
Hath this extent, no more.

His next speech begins with ethos. Othello is describing himself; a soldier since the age of seven, who is more used to the action of the battlefield than speaking in self-defence.

Rude am I in my speech
And little blessed with the soft phrase of peace;
For since these arms of mine had seven years' pith
Till now some nine moons wasted, they have used
Their dearest action in the tented field;
And little of this great world can I speak
More than pertains to feats of broil and battle:
And therefore little shall I grace my cause
In speaking for myself.

Finally – after an interlude offering a little more logos, peppered with facts about his relationship with Desdemona's father – comes the crux of the speech. With intense pathos, he recounts telling the father of his former life:

Wherein I spake of most disastrous chances,
Of moving accidents by flood and field,
Of hair-breadth scapes i' th'imminent deadly breach.
Of being taken by the insolent foe,

Sold to slavery; of my redemption thence,
And portance in my traveler's history:
Wherein of antres vast and deserts idle,
Rough quarries, rocks, and hills whose heads touch heaven,
It was my hint to speak – such was the process:
And of the Cannibals that each other eat,
The Anthropophagi, and men whose heads
Do grow beneath their shoulders.

He has led armies, faced danger, been captured, escaped and brought home spoils, all for Venice. He feels his deeds give him high enough standing to marry the daughter of a senator. The result is that the Duke of Venice is moved also: 'I think this tale would win my daughter too', he says.

The result of this work for the actor playing Othello was transformative. Understanding how specifically the character used these rhetorical strategies, allowed him to take the senators – and us – through Othello's story with control, and to reveal the eloquence of Othello's persuasive tactics.

One need not be delivering a Shakespearean oration to draw upon all three methods in this manner. If you are preparing a presentation, a motivational speech, or perhaps simply an idea you want to put forward at a team meeting, it can be helpful to use these three strategies consciously. Say you're making a sales pitch. Ethos could offer the detailed research you have done to make you really understand the idea or product and how you personally connect to it, perhaps finding a story about that research to illustrate your point. Logos would lie in the facts: further research which demonstrates the many practical or financial benefits the product or idea will bring to the group, the company or the success of the mission. Pathos might then be your conclusion, where you could excite your listeners as to the potential of your plan or your product – to make them feel good about its benefits to them, their organisation, their team or their buyers. Again, using a story or narrative about how the benefits might play out would be a great way to use this strategy. Pathos is an appeal to the imagination of your listeners. Through a story you can take them into the rosy future you are foretelling.

As you are putting together your piece, try this exercise:

Exercise 1: Ethos, logos and pathos

Take three blank pages and head each with the three different strategies. Under each heading, write how you might steer your information in the direction of the strategy.

- Under **ethos**, you might relate some appropriate personal history that connects to your argument; you might establish some common ground between yourself and your listeners; and you might present how you gained detailed knowledge of the issue, argument or product.

- Under **logos**, you might present the financial or other benefits of your argument or product; you might present the results of research into its potential; you might present the reasoning behind your ideas and any deductions you have made based on your research.

- Under **pathos**, you might use individual examples of the need for your product or idea; you might use a real or hypothetical narrative to illustrate how it could change the future of those it affects; and you might show how it might strengthen the standing or reputation of the company or team that initiates it.

When you put the whole piece together, you don't have to use the strategies in the order I have given you, and you might use each more than once. But make sure your focus is on getting the benefit of your idea, argument or product into the minds and hearts of your listeners. To do so, when practising, it can be helpful to speak the name of each strategy you are using before you move on to it. This could help you to be clear about the shifts, but also make you more aware that you are talking to individuals, and that the reason for the strategies is to really connect with them – not as a group or a company but as people.

The power of these methods is not limited to formal speeches and presentations, however. Once you are familiar with these rhetorical strategies, you will also find it quite simple to use them in your day-to-day exchanges, whether in an anecdote or perhaps a political debate. Using these strategies is a very effective way of engaging your listeners and drawing them closer into your argument.

STORYTELLING

Most people intuitively understand the power of storytelling as a way to get a message across. It is common to hear politicians telling the stories of people they have met (true or otherwise) to illustrate their points. Or consider a best man telling anecdotes about the groom's past at a wedding. But the power of storytelling reaches its zenith in the theatre. Following how characters' stories play out and considering their emotions is the heart of the business, perhaps even helping us to navigate and manage events in our own lives. As Lucian Msamati puts it: 'We learn the business of life through stories.' And this is where theatre is unique. 'It doesn't necessarily matter who, what or why the characters are, we are interested in their journey and what lesson they learn,' he says. 'Are they going to get their comeuppance in the end; am I going to have my values reaffirmed or smashed?'

However, for the listeners to engage strongly with a story, whether on stage, in a church or at a sales pitch, it is important that it is structured well. Recall the young woman in the National Theatre's finance team: the first thing I did to help her was to find in her speech the basic structure of all good storytelling – a beginning, a middle and an end; an introduction, an exploration and a con-clusion. Consider any classic fairy story: once upon a time . . . this is what happened . . . they all lived hap-pily ever after. Or an essay or thesis: say what you are going to say, say it, and then say you've said it. (The fairy story is perhaps more exciting than the essay and thesis examples, because in fairy stories we are allowed to dis-cover something; we are not told at the beginning what will happen at the end.) It is up to you to choose which style is most appropriate for your situation. Do you keep your revelations to the end, or do you let the audience know what you concluded at the beginning, and then show them how you got there?

This three-part structure is also one I always look for, and listen for, in speeches and in plays. In fact, I can hear those three parts in many plays, even when an actor hasn't found them themselves. When you look you can find it in almost all of Shakespeare's big speeches, and even in speeches of just a few lines. Consider the famous soliloquy in *Hamlet*, Act 3, Scene 1. Hamlet's father, the King of Denmark, has died, and his mother has married Claudius, his father's brother, within a month of the death. Claudius has also inherited the Kingdom. Hamlet has met the ghost of his father who tells him he was murdered by his brother and that Hamlet should avenge the murder. Hamlet has already told us that the act of revenge required of him is not in his nature. Now he is contemplating which is braver: to take his own life or live to carry out the dreaded deed he has promised to commit. And his famous opening lines are a classic *introduction*, raising the two choices he thinks he has:

> To be, or not to be, that is the question,
> Whether 'tis nobler in the mind to suffer
> The slings and arrows of outrageous fortune,
> Or to take arms against a sea of troubles,
> And by opposing end them?

Next comes a more detailed *exploration* of these options. He tells us about those choices, comparing the fear of 'The undiscovered country from whose bourn / No traveller returns' (death) to the 'whips and scorns of time' (life), but he doesn't come to a decision. When I'm working with an actor on a speech like this, after the introduction I might say 'tell me more about that'. Then the actor sees that he is developing or exploring the premise of his argument.

He finally concludes his meditation with:

Thus conscience does make cowards of us all
And thus the native hue of resolution
Is sicklied o'er with the pale cast of thought,
And enterprises of great pith and moment
With this regard their currents turn awry
And lose the name of action.

Although in this speech Hamlet does not appear to have reached a conclusion about the dilemma he has introduced, he does conclude that asking the question in the first place and debating it has stopped him from taking action. The conclusion of any piece should return to the argument put forward in the introduction.

Or take another speech you might be familiar with, or at least its first line. *The Merchant of Venice* takes up another of Shakespeare's great interests: the conflict between moral justice and legal justice. This speech is spoken by Portia, the play's heroine, in Act 4, Scene 1. She is disguised as a young male lawyer, or clerk, as she is described in the play. Shylock is a moneylender and Portia speaks in the case he has brought against Bassanio, a Venetian merchant to whom he has lent money. Shylock wants to claim the bond of security Bassanio has given him against the loan, which Bassanio has been unable to pay. The bond is a pound of flesh to be cut from near the heart. Portia begins:

The quality of mercy is not strain'd,
It droppeth as the gentle rain from heaven
Upon the place beneath.

She then goes on to explore the meaning of *mercy* when it is in the hands of the powerful, like Shylock (in this situation) and the judge in the court. She concludes:

We do pray for mercy,
And that same prayer doth teach us all to render
The deeds of mercy.

This simple structure gives a clear journey through the thoughts expressed and makes the arguments easy to follow: introduction, exploration and conclusion.

Even if you are not writing a speech from scratch – or are simply expressing yourself without a script in everyday conversation – it can be helpful to think about this structure. Using it in a spoken context solves a problem I often come across when working on clarity of thought and delivery with both actors and non-actors: 'What the heck are you talking about?' When no structure is in place, it is often hard to understand what point is being made, moment by moment. This tripartite structure gives you the opportunity to clearly and confidently state your premise, and it is important that you do so for the rest of your argument to be listened to and understood.

The following exercise will help you find a tripartite structure in your own address.

Exercise 2: To find the three-part structure of arguments

Place three chairs in a triangular formation in a room with some space between them. Stand in the middle of the triangle with the script of your speech. Walk to one of the chairs and sit on it. When you are sitting on it read the introduction to your piece. When you get to the end of your introduction, get up and walk in silence to another chair and sit on it. Then read the exploration (the middle section of your piece), however long it is. When you have finished that, get up, walk in silence to the third chair and sit on that. Then read the conclusion of your piece.

Part of this exercise is to find out exactly where these three sections are. Working through the speech in this way will help you to decide if you are clear about where they begin and end.

When you have done the whole exercise, stand and read the whole speech through again, in the light of the exercise. Did your structure work? Did it help you to lay out your argument as a journey? Did it help you to keep your thinking tight?

You can also find a beginning, middle and end within each specific point that you make. Try repeating this exercise with the central (exploration) section of your piece: can you find further introductions, explorations and conclusions here too? As you move from chair to chair to dissect each point, you may notice that some sections aren't clear and need rewriting. Maybe you will see that some sections work without this structure or maybe stand out because their structure is different: a simple statement of fact, for example, or a rhetorical question that you could choose to answer or not. When you have finished the exercise, stand and read the whole exploration section again in the light of the exercise. Is each point clear?

When you have a clear view of the three parts of your overall speech, and any three parts of the various points you make within your argument, you can test that you have kept on track by just reading the beginnings and the ends. Start with the introduction, then read the conclusion, missing out the exploration. If it makes sense, then you know you are being clear. You can see it in the two Shakespeare speeches I showed you – I didn't give you the middle sections but the beginnings and ends I have provided make perfect sense when read together.

Working with the three-part structure forces you to be clear about what you are saying, and when your thoughts and your reasoning are clear you can lay out your stall and make each point confidently. Finding and using the three-part structure can put you firmly in control of your argument, your intention and your audience.

EPISODES, FACTS AND EVENTS

Both Aristotle's strategies and the tripartite storytelling journey are rhetorical devices that I use with actors to define helpful structures within debates, arguments and stories. But there is another method that directors and actors commonly use during a play's rehearsal, which helps identify the implicit structure of a piece of writing. Once again, it is a model based on the ideas of Stanislavski and his followers.

Usually, the first week of a rehearsal period is spent on analysis of the text of the play. The actors, director and sometimes other members of the creative team, such as voice and movement coaches, will sit around a table and carefully work through the whole play. The aim is that the acting company should all have the same view of the play and a common purpose in bringing it to life. In establishing this method, Stanislavski wanted to create a rehearsal process through which the actors felt involved in the whole story, knowing what part each character plays in the arc of the narrative. This might seem unsurprising to us, but Stanislavski had entered an acting profession that was very different from today's; rehearsals were minimal, and the concerns of individual actors were given priority over the play as a whole. The style of performance was to present the play out to the audience, using strong physical and facial gestures, rather than to play naturally to other characters within the scene.

In order for the company to have a strong sense of the development of the plot and the journey of the characters within the play, Stanislavski first introduced the idea of dividing the play into a series of *beats* – or 'bits', as he called them. Stanislavski often referred to the text of a play as a *score* and there are many hints that his method of textual analysis was influenced by the analysis of a musical score. In rehearsals today, these divisions are commonly called *units*. These beats or units chart the forward movement of the narrative and mark where dramatic changes occur. As Christopher Saul recalls of his experience during one of his seasons at the Royal Shakespeare Company, 'If it's a theatre script, more often than not the entirety will be split into sections,' he tells me. 'On the first day of rehearsals for *Imperium*' – a dramatisation of the opening book of Robert Harris's Cicero trilogy – 'we sat, read and volunteered titles for each scene or sections of scene.'

According to Stanislavski, the beats change when there is a change in the circumstances, activity or atmosphere within a scene or the whole play. As his work progressed, he developed the idea or beats into more specific episodes, events and facts. To see how this works in practice, consider a famous scene from *Romeo and Juliet*, in which the lovers first meet at a masked ball held in the house of Juliet's family, the Capulets, enemies to Romeo's family, the Montagues.

According to Stanislavski's method, this scene could by itself be considered an *episode* in the story as a whole; it is when Romeo and Juliet first meet and discover they come from warring families. As such, it is one of the larger building blocks of the story of this tragedy.

Within the scene there are these smaller dramatic *events*:

- Juliet's father welcomes guests to the ball and encourages everyone to dance.
- Romeo and his friends arrive.
- They are recognised by Juliet's cousin Tybalt who reports the fact to her father who then tells him not to challenge Romeo.
- Romeo and Juliet meet.
- They discover they are from opposing families, and the Montague boys exit speedily.

Meanwhile, the *facts* we discover in the scene are these:

- That the last time the two families were on familiar terms was about thirty years ago.

- That Romeo is about twenty-five.
- That Tybalt is a fiery character who when he is restrained by Juliet's father, vows that it will make him more determined to fight the Montagues.

Finally, you could consider that there are some distinct changes in the *atmosphere* of the scene, which begins in festive, party mood but changes:

- When the angry Tybalt speaks to Juliet's father.
- When the lovers meet.
- When they discover they are from opposing families.

This division of a script offers a useful way to plan any piece of verbal communication. It could help you to pace the speech and to make sure each element is clearly defined and presented. It might also help you to be particularly persuasive if you recognise that you can change the atmosphere in the room by how you speak.

Consider a political speech. Here is Abraham Lincoln's famous 'Gettysburg Address', delivered on 19 November 1863. He begins with a *fact*:

Four score and seven years ago our fathers brought forth on this continent, a new nation, conceived in Liberty, and dedicated to the proposition that all men are created equal.

He then moves to an *event*, what is happening now:

> *Now we are engaged in a great civil war, testing whether that nation or any nation so conceived and so dedicated, can long endure.*

He follows this with more *facts*:

> *We are met on a great battle-field of that war. We have come to dedicate a portion of that field, as a final resting place for those who here gave their lives that that nation might live. It is altogether fitting and proper that we should do this.*

Then an *event* – what we would like to do but has already been done.

> *But in a larger sense, we can not dedicate – we can not consecrate – we can not hallow – this ground. The brave men, living and dead, who struggled here, have consecrated it, far above our poor power to add or detract.*

Then another *fact*:

> *The world will little note, nor long remember what we say here, but it can never forget what they did here.*

He finishes with an *event* – what we must do:

It is for us the living, rather, to be dedicated here to the unfinished work which they who fought here have thus far so nobly advanced. It is rather for us to be here dedicated to the great task remaining before us – that from these honored dead we take increased devotion to that cause for which they gave the last full measure of devotion – that we here highly resolve that these dead shall not have died in vain – that this nation, under God, shall have a new birth of freedom – and that government of the people, by the people, for the people, shall not perish from the earth.

These shifts from facts to events change the atmosphere of the speech. The facts are firm, but the events are charged with emotion as Lincoln reflects on the heroism and sacrifice of their forebears and his determination that the future should honour the declaration of Liberty for all.

One need not be making a speech as formal as the Gettysburg Address to find these characteristics. Try this exercise to see if you can use this structure to tell a story.

Exercise 3: Finding facts, events and atmosphere

In this exercise we are going to tell the following story: you are at a wedding reception, and you are introduced to the potential partner of your dreams. You stand up to greet them and knock food and drink all over them and yourself. You can then decide how

---

it plays out after that. Imagine this is one episode in the overall story of the wedding, or your relationship: it might lead to another episode, when you meet again in the washroom perhaps, or at another social or work event.

In this episode, you might describe the following facts:

- You are friends with one or both of the married couple.
- You have drunk too much.
- You don't know the prospective partner.
- The prospective partner could be a friend or relative of a friend.
- You can add other facts to embellish the story.

The events might be as follows:

- You are eating, perhaps with fellow guests.
- The introduction is made.
- You stand up and drop the food or drink and maybe make an attempt to clean up.
- Other events occur as a consequence of that mishap.

Now put this together in a story.

1. Set up the episode at the wedding.
2. Tell us the facts in a narrative.

3. Describe the events in as much detail and humour as you like.

4. Include the changes in atmosphere that come about when the introduction is made, and then when the mishap occurs. That could be how you feel when you see the other person, how that changes when you drop the food/drink and how others react to the event and your behaviour. This will be the icing on the cake of your story.

Then continue in this way as you develop the story to a conclusion. Like the actors, you could choose a title for the episode and the events that occur within it, to help you focus your ideas and remember the details.

Learning to spot episodes, facts and events can be a useful way of preparing a presentation or a speech, as it makes you mindful of what effect each moment will have on the story you tell. But it could just as readily be applied to an anecdote, a joke or even just a single point in a conversation. Even better, this tool can be easily combined with the other methods in this chapter – including ethos, logos and pathos and the tripartite storytelling structure. The more familiar you are with these methods, the more dexterously you will be able to use them.

THE IMPORTANCE OF LISTENING

Rhetoric works best when it emphasises not only talking but also listening. When you are listening properly to other people's arguments, you will have more chance of countering theirs with your own. Remember the first lines of Brutus' and Antony's speeches? Antony listened very carefully to Brutus' argument and was able to take what he had said and turn it to his own advantage by using the same words but rephrasing them. In doing so, he emphasised the difference between himself and Brutus and reached out into the hearts and imaginations of his listeners. Hearing Brutus' logos, he countered with ethos and pathos. In any debate or argument, listening is crucial for you to be able to steer the course in the direction you want it to go.

Similarly, if you are telling a story or joke or giving a sermon, lecture or presentation, you need to be able to listen to your audience; to be aware of whether they are listening to you or not. Actors often talk about *hearing* their audience. Even when they are in the midst of a scene, they will often have a sense of how the audience is reacting. Are they with them, are they listening intently, or are they coughing or shifting about a lot? They can use what they hear to determine whether they are playing at the right pace and rhythm. This awareness is important to anyone who is speaking, whether to a big audience or to one or two friends.

If you feel you are losing your listeners' attention, you can change your strategy or bring in a story event to enliven your piece. Othello began his defence with an apologetic ethos: this is who I am, an honest, simple soldier. He then moved to logos, stating the truth of the fact that he had married Desdemona. But it was when he switched to pathos, using descriptive, sometimes metaphorical language to tell the story of his life, that he won his listeners round. In a recent National Theatre production of this play, with Giles Terera in the title role, the director, Clint Dyer, chose to emphasise this point in the staging. At first, the members of the senate interrupt Othello's speeches with boos and jeers. As he hears this, we see him change tack as it's clear they are not responding to his first two strategies. Then we see that the listeners begin to pay attention as they are drawn into his stories. By listening intently, Othello is able to win his audience around.

Throughout this book, my emphasis and that of the actors I interviewed has been on thinking about your audience as *listeners*. We know that our work exists not for our own benefit, to gain praise and fame, but to get into the ears and imaginations of our audiences. To tell them stories; to show them lives, experiences and opinions that may not be their own, but which could change them. We know that we have to make sure our audience hear us, and it is easier to hear and understand a well-written and well-structured play.

This is true for anyone who needs to communicate in any setting. Your thoughts, arguments and propositions will be more persuasive if they are well structured and delivered with a clear aim in view. The result is true eloquence: inspiring, fluent, persuasive speaking.

LAST WORD

I once asked Lucian Msamati what he felt was the most important element of his work. 'The word that pops up immediately is craft,' he said. 'Which for me is ever-evolving, never-ending, and it's a combination of discipline, rigour, joy, fun, but also the danger of the spontaneous moment; the brilliance of a happy accident. But you can't get to happy accidents if you haven't been rigorous and disciplined before.'

This focus on disciplined preparation was mentioned by almost every actor featured in this book. As we have seen in each chapter, it is through hard work that actors ensure their voices and their bodies are in shape for the rigours of live theatre performances; they rehearse thoroughly and they study their scripts to be sure of the rhetoric and to have a clear understanding of the intentions and actions of the characters they are playing. In preparing so rigorously, actors, directors, voice coaches and everyone who works closely with the text of a play are continually exploring the lives, society and psyche of other people.

And they are looking at themselves, too. We have seen how actors in training are encouraged to reflect upon themselves closely to have understanding of and empathy for the characters in plays. In theatre we live examined lives; physical, psychological and emotional exploration is our stock in trade. This close, sympathetic examination also means the actor is continually aware of how life impinges on the body and the voice.

Things do go wrong, of course. In 2015, when in his early eighties, Patrick Godfrey played the central role in Caryl Churchill's play *Here We Go*. He opened the second section of the play with an extraordinary, very long monologue, where his character is seemingly at the very point of death. On the play's first public performance, Patrick tells me, he 'dried' in the middle of the monologue – that is, he forgot his next line. 'It happened because I got a laugh and I wasn't prepared for that,' he recalls. 'It completely threw me.' He remembers shaking with fear when it happened. 'When we were young, we didn't shake with fear . . . we thought we were so wonderful,' he laughs. 'When you're getting on a bit you realise you're not wonderful at all – anything can go wrong.' (Of course, he was wonderful!)

Many of the actors I spoke to for this book have described similar experiences. Debra Gillett told me that she has been on stage when sets have collapsed and actors have forgotten their lines, that there have been moments when she had the giggles, moments when she dropped lines. She said that when these things happen 'time stands still and you feel totally exposed'.

In the course of your own performances, you will inevitably have moments like these. The solution is not to try to eliminate all errors – but instead to respond in the right way. Simon Trinder recounts a performance of an RSC production of *The Tempest* at the Barbican Theatre in which he was playing Trinculo; he was in the middle of a comedy scene, and he suddenly felt that something that usually got a laugh hadn't landed. He began to tell himself off internally for what he felt was a failure. But then he realised that this was exactly the problem. 'Most of my fear and anxiety and nerves are wrapped up in getting it right,' he observes. 'That's where the tension comes from, physically and vocally . . . It's where the frozen thinking comes from, when you're not able to respond impulsively – you're stuck in your head.' At that moment he realised that he was never going to be 100 per cent perfect and that he should allow himself '10 per cent of terrible'; a revelation that gave him the freedom to be good.

This is as good a place as any to end the book. Over the last five chapters, we have learned how you get the best out of yourself, physically and vocally, and by so doing you enhance your authenticity. We have explored how to achieve authority without arrogance when speaking at work or in your social life. We have touched upon rhetoric and storytelling to develop eloquent, persuasive language. And we have discovered how, when we put them together, these three components lead to truly charismatic communication. You may now be thinking, with so much information, where do I start? How do I choose the right exercises for me? Which methods will help me to get my message across, tell my story, amuse my friends, or get me the job or the promotion?

To begin with, I suggest you take time and care over Chapters 1 and 2. Not only do your physical habits affect your voice, but your self-awareness and the way you present yourself physically can have a big impact on how people relate to you – and hear you. If you really want to improve your vocal skills, be prepared to do the breathing and voice exercises regularly, maybe as a routine alongside any physical exercises you do. You will soon hear positive changes.

Everything else you need will build upon these exercises. Having confidence in your own authority will come through a combination of how you apply your vocal skills to your presentations, speeches and conversations, and how you engage with your listeners. So, the work in Chapters 3 and 4 are part of your ongoing exercise work – as well as offering a new way of thinking about how you communicate. It will be useful to set yourself some practice time on any scripts or texts you need to deliver, as well as beginning to be aware of your active listening and speaking skills. You should also start to consider how best to own a room; something you can think about – and learn – even when you aren't on stage.

Which leads on to the work on rhetoric and storytelling. This can become a fundamental way of structuring your thoughts and ideas. The more you study and practise the techniques I have outlined in Chapter 5, the more obvious and instinctive they will become. You can combine them, or choose particular ways of getting your points across, depending on the material you are drawing upon. This deep, considered work on yourself and your communication skills will pay off – and you will eventually develop your own style of charismatic communication.

Just remember that, however much you prepare, inevitably things will go wrong. And that is not something to be feared. As Simon Trinder puts it: 'Don't go for perfection, go for excellence – and then you'll get somewhere.'

Excellence, after all, is something that can for the most part be learned. With attention and courage, anyone can take centre stage.

ACKNOWLEDGEMENTS

My grateful thanks to Rowan Borchers who commissioned, guided and edited this book with grace, patience and good humour. Thanks to Katya Browne and all the team at Cornerstone Press/Penguin Random House, including Ceara Elliot, Isabelle Ralphs and Lydia Weigel. Also, many thanks to Harry Scoble, Sarah Corke and Zara Jayant at the National Theatre.

Most of all, my thanks to the actors who agreed to be interviewed for the book: Peter Forbes, Danny Sapani, Lucian Msamati, Tamsin Greig, Adjoa Andoh, Debra Gillett, Patrick Godfrey, Mark Gatiss, Simon Trinder, Justine Mitchell, Nathalie Armin, Christopher Saul, Deborah Findlay and Niamh Cusack.

ABOUT THE AUTHOR

Jeannette Nelson is one of the world's leading voice coaches. During her twenty-five years as Head of Voice at the National Theatre, she was responsible for ensuring that everyone who took the stage at Britain's leading theatre was communicating clearly and charismatically. Along the way, she worked with some of the greatest actors of our time – from Al Pacino to Ralph Fiennes to Juliette Binoche – on some of their most notable roles across stage, film and TV. Jeannette's previous books, *The Voice Exercise Book* (2015) and *Keeping it Active* (2022), have become the go-to resources for actors looking to improve their communication skills; in *Centre Stage*, she introduces this work to a popular audience for the first time.